LEISURE THE BASIS OF CULTURE

~

THE PHILOSOPHICAL ACT

JOSEF PIEPER

LEISURE
THE BASIS OF CULTURE

THE PHILOSOPHICAL ACT

TRANSLATED BY ALEXANDER DRU

IGNATIUS PRESS   SAN FRANCISCO

Cover photograph by
© Christina Hanck/istockphoto

Cover design by Roxanne Mei Lum

Foreword © 2009 by Ignatius Press, San Francisco
All rights reserved
ISBN 978-1-58617-256-5 (PB)
ISBN 978-1-68149-291-9 (eBook)
Library of Congress Control Number 2007942856
Printed in the United States of America ∞

CONTENTS

LEISURE THE BASIS OF CULTURE

THE PHILOSOPHICAL ACT

FOREWORD
BY JAMES V. SCHALL, S.J.

When a culture is in the process of denying its own roots, it becomes most important to know what these roots are. We had best know what we reject before we reject it. If we are going to build a chair, the first thing we need to know, above all else, is what a chair is. Otherwise, we can do nothing. We are not a culture that never understood what a human being was in his nature and in his destiny.

Rather we are a culture that, having once known these things, has decided against living them or understanding them. Indeed, we have decided to reject most of them, almost as an act of defiance—as an act of pure humanism—as if what we are is not first given to us. We have let an empty future that we propose to make by our own standards become the ideal over and against a real past that revealed to us what man really was and is: namely, a being open to wonder who did not create himself or the world in which he dwells.

This little book by the German philosopher Josef Pieper is simply a gem. No book its size will teach us so many true things about everything we need to know to understand what and why we are or about how to live a life worth living. This book is one of the first I recommend for waking us up to what life is all about, to what is essential to and glorious about our lives. Pieper, through his writing, gives us the quiet assurance that he knows what is important. He has an uncanny command over the way to bring reality to our attention in a manner that makes it ours yet leaves it as it is.

This book contains two related essays that Pieper gave in Bonn in 1947. The first is on the classic notion of "leisure", what we "do" when all else—politics, economics, daily duties—is done. The second essay is on what it means to philosophize. Augustine said that there is "no other reason for men to philosophize but to be happy". Pieper would agree with this. The second essay is often overlooked, but it contains the profoundest insights about the nature of philosophy, its self-understanding, and its relation to theology.

Both essays belong together. Man has the power to know *all that is*. This is what his mind gives him. Yet he still knows himself as a finite being by knowing what is not himself. This is the importance of the philosophic life. It is for its own sake; yea, it is even "useless" because it is not for something else other than its own delight in knowing the truth. No short essay will teach the reader what his knowing powers are about better than Pieper's "Philosophic Act". Few have ever had such an act explained at all, let alone so well.

Originally, these essays were written with the background of World War II and its aftermath. Here, Pieper was already quite aware that the first principle of action is the end for which we act. If we get this source of action wrong, our efforts to achieve our end will go wrong. When read today, these essays now stand against the background not only of World War II and then of the decline of Marxism, but also of the absolutization of democracy and the resurrection of Islam. A world once thought to be automatically prosperous is suddenly thrown back on its essentials.

At first sight, it seems that something, almost anything, must be done about our situation. But it is the genius of Pieper to see that this activist, busy motion is the wrong starting point. Before we can pretend to do anything about the present, we must know what we are, what the world is, and yes, what God is. Construction of a civilization that knows little or nothing of these deeper realities can only make things worse.

In a world in which German writers are not always known as models of clarity, Josef Pieper writes with a concise, comprehensible style. In the briefest manner, his writings always show his familiarity with the great thinkers of our tradition. He does not always agree with them, but he always learns from both their mistakes and their insights. He tells what each is. Pieper does not begin with modernity and the presumption that what the classics and medievals held made no difference. Indeed, knowing little or nothing before Machiavelli or Descartes is a formula for philosophical incoherence. In a surprising way, every book of Pieper's is a short treatise on the whole of philosophy and its history. In his writings, Pieper is a great teacher, even for the beginner. His audiences are those eager to find the truth, indeed those eager to know that there is a truth. Pieper is the great antidote to philosophical skepticism and to sophistry in every form.

What is at issue in the word "leisure", a famous Greek word from which we get the word "school", is both an inner worldly and a transcendent understanding of the highest things. Following Aristotle, we realize that something "divine" lies in our knowing of *what is*. We are not simply to devote ourselves to politics and economics or to making a living, however valid these are in their own spheres. Pieper is quite aware of these things as elements in human life. But he recognizes that when everything human is defined in terms of utility or pleasure, the enterprise of knowing what we are loses its centrality in our lives. There are things beyond politics and without which politics cannot be politics.

Pieper is remarkably good in explaining to us that our minds are open to a reality that is not ourselves; in fact we stand in wonder and amazement at what is not ourselves. Much modern science has tried to tell us that there is nothing "out there" to find. All we do, it is said, is "project" ourselves. Pieper will have none of this blindness. He understands the shortcomings of an epistemology that would close us off from reality, including our own reality. More importantly, he makes us aware that we stand in a gift relation to what is not ourselves. What is closer to our existence is not the power we project out onto the world but the reality itself that is a gift to us. About reality we wonder how we should be grateful and to whom.

Pieper's famous little book is a short philosophy course discovered by those fortunate few who read him, a book often found by chance. This book exists in a world that knows little of philosophy as it was originally understood —as a love of wisdom, a love of *what is*. None of us are gods who presumably are already wise: we are but men who wonder, who seek to know for no other reason than the knowing itself.

Pieper is amazing in the way that he finds brief, pithy statements about his point from Aquinas, Plato, Goethe, Aristotle, and others. From *Disputed Questions on the Virtues* by Aquinas, Pieper is fond of saying that contemplative life is not properly human but superhuman. St. Thomas even says that *homo naturaliter non est humanus sed superhumanus est*, so that things that are human point to what is beyond human nature. Pieper understands that this reality of man's actual being impinges on our lives and thought in such a way that, by being what we are, we become both better philosophers and better human beings.

Leisure the Basis of Culture and *The Philosophical Act* are together very brief. Together they cannot be matched as an introduction and explication of what we are. They teach us the two greatest things about ourselves: that we did not cause ourselves to be and that we cannot but be amazed and grateful that what we are actually exists in our own persons and in the companions we find in this mortal life, itself destined not just to itself but to eternal life. Other books may also teach us this, but no book will do it quite so well.

—James V. Schall, S.J.
Department of Government
Georgetown University
Lent, 2009

AUTHOR'S PREFACE
TO THE ENGLISH EDITION

These two essays were published separately in Germany, the second having been originally written in the form of lectures, given in Bonn in the summer of 1947. They are intimately connected and properly belong together. This is not only true in the sense that they were both written in the same summer, in a single breath, so to say; they both spring from the same thought.

Their common origin or foundation might be stated in the following words: Culture depends for its very existence on leisure, and leisure, in its turn, is not possible unless it has a durable and consequently living link with the *cultus*, with divine worship.

The word "cult" in English is used exclusively, or almost exclusively, in a derivative sense. But here it is used, along with worship, in its primary sense. It means something else than, and something more than, religion. It really means fulfilling the ritual of public sacrifice. That is a notion which contemporary "modern" man associates almost exclusively and unconsciously with uncivilized, primitive peoples and with classical antiquity. For that very reason it is of the first importance to see that the *cultus*, now as in the distant past, is the primary source of man's freedom, independence and immunity within society. Suppress that last sphere of freedom, and freedom itself, and all our liberties, will in the end vanish into thin air.

Culture, in the sense in which it is used above, is the quintessence of all the natural goods of the world and of those gifts and qualities which, while belonging to man, lie beyond the immediate sphere of his needs and wants. All that is good in this sense, all man's gifts and faculties are not necessarily useful in a practical way; though there is no denying that they belong to a truly human life, not strictly speaking necessary, even though he could not do without them.

Among the *bona non utilia sed honesta* which are at home in the realm of freedom, in its innermost circle indeed, is philosophy, the philosophical act, which must be understood in the traditional sense of Plato, Aristotle, Augustine and Aquinas, and as they understood it. Grant this original sense of the word "philosophizing" to be the true one, and it is no longer possible to speak of the philosophical aspect in the same way that one might speak of a sociological and historical or a political aspect—as though one could take up the one or the other at will. In the tradition of which I am speaking, the philosophical act is a fundamental relation to reality, a full, personal attitude which is by no manner of means at the sole disposal of the *ratio*; it is an attitude which presupposes silence, a contemplative attention to things, in which man begins to see how worthy of veneration they really are. And it is perhaps only in this way that it is possible to understand how it was that Plato's philosophical school, the Academy in Athens, was at the same time a sort of club or society for the celebration of the *cultus*. In the last resort pure theory, philosophical *theoria*, entirely free from practical considerations and interference—and that is what theory is—can only be preserved and realized within the sphere of leisure, and leisure, in its turn, is free because of its relation to worship, to the *cultus*.

LEISURE
THE BASIS OF CULTURE

But the gods, taking pity on mankind, born to work, laid down the succession of recurring Feasts to restore them from their fatigue, and gave them the Muses, and Apollo their leader, and Dionysus, as companions in their Feasts, so that nourishing themselves in festive companionship with the gods, they should again stand upright and erect.

PLATO

Be still and know that I am God.

PSALM 46:10

I

Let me begin with an objection, an objection of the kind
which the scholastics called a *Videtur quod non*. Now of all
times, in the post-war years is not the time to talk about
leisure. We are, after all, busy building our house. Our hands
are full and there is work for all. And surely, until our task
is done and our house is rebuilt, the only thing that matters
is to strain every nerve.

That is not an objection to be put lightly aside. And yet,
whenever our task carries us beyond the maintenance of
a bare existence and the satisfaction of our most pressing
needs, once we are faced with reorganizing our intellectual
and moral and spiritual assets—then, before discussing the
problem in detail, a fresh start and new foundations call for
a defense of leisure.

For assuming all too rashly, for the moment, that our new
house is going to be built in the Western tradition—a thing
so arguable that it might almost be said to be the decision
which is hanging in the balance—it is essential to begin
by reckoning with the fact that one of the foundations of
Western culture is leisure. That much, at least, can be learnt
from the first chapter of Aristotle's *Metaphysics*. And even
the history of the word attests the fact: for leisure in Greek
is *skole*, and in Latin *scola*, the English "school". The word

The quotation preceding the essay is from the *Laws* (653 C-d). The psalm
is translated from the Septuagint; it begins with the word σχολάσατε. It has
been said by Joseph Bernhardt that this verse "became an axiom of mystical
epistemology."

used to designate the place where we educate and teach is derived from a word which means "leisure". "School" does not, properly speaking, mean school, but leisure.

The original conception of leisure, as it arose in the civilized world of Greece, has, however, become unrecognizable in the world of planned diligence and "total labor"; and in order to gain a clear notion of leisure we must begin by setting aside the prejudice—our prejudice—that comes from overvaluing the sphere of work. In his well-known study of capitalism Max Weber[1] quotes the saying, that "one does not work to live; one lives to work", which nowadays no one has much difficulty in understanding: it expresses the current opinion. We even find some difficulty in grasping that it reverses the order of things and stands them on their head.

But what ought we to say to the opposite view, to the view that "we work in order to have leisure"? We should not hesitate to say that here indeed "the world of topsy-turvydom", the world that had been stood on its head, has been clearly expressed. To those who live in a world of nothing but work, in what we might call the world of "total work", it presumably sounds immoral, as though directed at the very foundations of human society.

That maxim is not, however, an illustration invented for the sake of clarifying this thesis: it is a quotation from Aristotle; and the fact that it expresses the view of a cool-headed workaday realist (as he is supposed to have been) gives it all the more weight. Literally, the Greek says "we are unleisurely in order to have leisure."[2] "To be unleisurely"— that is the word the Greeks used not only for the daily toil

---

[1] In his well-known study on Capitalism and Protestant ethics, p. 171 (1934).

[2] *Nicomachean Ethics.*

and moil of life, but for ordinary everyday work. Greek only has the negative, *a-scolia*, just as Latin has *neg-otium*.

The context of Aristotle's words, and his other statement (in the *Politics*) to the effect that leisure is the center-point about which everything revolves,[3] seems to indicate that he was saying something almost self-evident; and one can only suppose that the Greeks would not have understood our maxims about "work for work's sake" at all. On the other hand it must be evident that we no longer understand their conception of leisure simply and directly.

This is perhaps the point at which to anticipate the objection: "What does Aristotle honestly matter to us? We may admire the world of antiquity, but why should we feel under any obligation to it?"

Among other things, it might be pointed out in reply that the Christian and Western conception of the contemplative life is closely linked to the Aristotelian notion of leisure. It is also to be observed that this is the source of the distinction between the *artes liberales* and the *artes serviles*, the liberal arts and servile work. And to the further objection that this distinction only interests historians, one might reply that everyone is familiar with at any rate one half of the distinction, from the fact that we still speak of "servile work" as unsuitable on Sundays and holidays. Though who nowadays stops to think that "servile work" and "liberal arts" are twin expressions, and form, one might almost say, the articulation of a joint, so that the one is hardly intelligible without the other? For it is barely possible to think of "servile work" with any degree of accuracy without delimiting the sense with reference to the "liberal arts".

All this, and much besides, might be adduced to show that

[3] *Politics*, 8, 3 (1337b).

Aristotle is more than a name; though it is true that purely historical considerations are no basis for an obligation.

But the immediate purpose was really to make it plain that the value we set on work and on leisure is very far from being the same as that of the Greek and Roman world, or of the Middle Ages, for that matter—so very different that the men of the past would have been incapable of understanding the modern conception of work, just as we are unable to understand their notion of leisure simply and directly, without an effort of thought. The tremendous difference of point of view implied and our relative ignorance of the notion of leisure emerge more clearly if we examine the notion of work in its modern form, spreading, as it does, to cover and include the whole of human activity and even of human life; for then we shall realize to what an extent we tacitly acknowledge the claims that are made in the name of the "worker".

Here and in all that follows "worker" must not be taken as defining an occupation, as in statistical works; it is *not* synonymous with "proletarian"—although the fact that the words are interchangeable is significant. On the contrary, "worker" will be used in an anthropological sense; it implies a whole conception of "man". Ernst Niekisch was using the word "worker" in this sense when he spoke of the "worker" as an "imperial figure";[4] and Ernst Jünger[5] uses the same term to outline the ideal image that, according to him, has already begun to mold the man of the future.

A new and changing conception of the nature of man, a new and changing conception of the very meaning of human existence—that is what comes to light in the claims

[4] Ernst Niekisch, *Die dritte imperiale Figur* (1935).
[5] Ernst Jünger, *Der Arbeiter. Herschaft und Gestalt* (1932).

expressed in the modern notion of "work" and "worker". These great subterranean changes in our scale of values, and in the meaning of value, are never easy to detect and lay bare, and they can certainly not be seen at a glance. And if we are to succeed in our purpose and uncover this great change, a historical treatment of the subject will be altogether inadequate; it becomes necessary to dig down to the roots of the problem and so base our conclusions on a philosophical and theological conception of man.

II

"Intellectual work" and "intellectual worker" are the sign-posts indicating the last stretch of the historical journey, a historical journey in the course of which the modern ideal of work was defined in its final and extreme form—for the terms are relatively modern.

Intellectual activity used always to be considered a privi-leged sphere, and from the standpoint of the manual worker especially, appeared to be a sphere in which one did not need to work. Within that sphere, the province of philosophy and of philosophical culture seemed furthest from the world of work. But nowadays the whole field of intellectual activ-ity, not excepting the province of philosophical culture, has been overwhelmed by the modern ideal of work and is at the mercy of its totalitarian claims. That is the latest phase of the struggle for power, of the process whereby that "im-perial figure" the "worker" seizes power. And this seizure of power reveals its challenge most clearly in the implicit claims underlying the notions of "intellectual work" and "intellectual worker".

The last stretch of the road has one advantage from the point of the spectator: it sums up the whole historical move-ment once again in a single formula of the utmost concision and clarity. The real meaning of the ideal of the world of "total work" reveals itself if one examines the inner struc-ture of the concept "intellectual work" and follows it down to its ultimate conclusions.

The concept of "intellectual work" may be traced back and explored in terms of various historical sources. It implies, in the first place, a very definite view of the mode and manner of man's intellectual knowledge. What happens when we look at a rose? What do we do as we become aware of color and form? Our soul is passive and receptive. We are, to be sure, awake and active, but our attention is not strained; we simply "look"—in so far, that is, as we "contemplate" it and are not already "observing" it (for "observing" implies that we are beginning to count, to measure and to weigh up). Observation is a tense activity; which is what Ernst Jünger meant when he called seeing an "act of aggression".[1] To contemplate, on the other hand, to "look" in this sense, means to open one's eyes receptively to whatever offers itself to one's vision, and the things seen enter into us, so to speak, without calling for any effort or strain on our part to possess them. There can hardly be any doubt that that, or something like it, is the way we become sensorially aware of a thing.

But what of knowledge, the mind's spiritual knowledge? Is there such a thing as a purely receptive attitude of mind in which we become aware of immaterial reality and invisible relationships? Is there such a thing as pure "intellectual contemplation"—to adopt the terminology of the schools? In antiquity the answer given was always yes; in modern philosophy, for the most part, the answer given is no.

Kant, for example, held knowledge to be exclusively "discursive": that is to say, the opposite of intuitive. "The reason cannot intuit anything."[2] His opinion on this point has quite recently been called "the most momentous dogmatic

[1] *Blätter und Steine*, p. 202 (1934).

[2] Immanuel Kant, *Kritik der reinen Vernunft*. Ed. by R. Schmidt (Leipzig, 1944), p. 95.

assumption of Kantian epistemology."[3] According to Kant man's knowledge is realized in the act of comparing, examining, relating, distinguishing, abstracting, deducing, demonstrating—all of which are forms of active intellectual effort. Knowledge, man's spiritual, intellectual knowledge (such is Kant's thesis) is activity, exclusively activity.

Working on that basis, Kant was bound to reach the view that knowing and philosophizing (philosophizing in particular, since it is furthest removed from purely physical awareness) must be regarded and understood as *work*. And lest there should be any doubt on the point he said so explicitly in an article written in 1796, against the romantic, contemplative and intuitive philosophy of Jacobi, Schlosser and Stolberg.[4] In philosophy, we read there, "the law is that reason acquires its possessions through work." The philosophy of the romantics is not genuine philosophy because it involves no work—a reproach that could, in some measure, be leveled at Plato himself, "the father of enthusiasm in philosophy"; "whereas", he continues, with reverent agreement, "the philosophy of Aristotle is work." Opinions, he says, such as those of the romantics, the sense that philosophy was above "work", have been responsible for "the new, superior tone in philosophy": a pseudo-philosophy "in which there is no need to work; one only has to attend to the oracle in one's breast and enjoy it, and so possess that wisdom whole and entire, which is the end of philosophy" —a pseudo-philosophy that thinks it can look down haughtily on the effort and work of the true philosopher. So much for Immanuel Kant.

[3] Bernhard Jansen, *Die Geschichte der Erkenntnislehre in der neueren Philosophie*, p. 235 (1940).

[4] "Von einem neuerdings erhobenen vornehmen Ton in der Philosophie." *Akademie-Ausgabe*, VIII, pp. 387–406.

The philosophers of antiquity thought otherwise on this matter—though of course their view is very far from offering grounds of justification for those who take the easy path. The Greeks—Aristotle no less than Plato—as well as the great medieval thinkers, held that not only physical, sensuous perception, but equally man's spiritual and intellectual knowledge, included an element of pure, receptive contemplation, or as Heraclitus says, of "listening to the essence of things".[5]

The Middle Ages drew a distinction between the understanding as *ratio* and the understanding as *intellectus*. *Ratio* is the power of discursive, logical thought, of searching and of examination, of abstraction, of definition and drawing conclusions. *Intellectus*, on the other hand, is the name for the understanding in so far as it is the capacity of *simplex intuitus*, of that simple vision to which truth offers itself like a landscape to the eye. The faculty of mind, man's knowledge, is both these things in one, according to antiquity and the Middle Ages, simultaneously *ratio* and *intellectus*; and the process of knowing is the action of the two together. The mode of discursive thought is accompanied and impregnated by an effortless awareness, the contemplative vision of the *intellectus*, which is not active but passive, or rather receptive, the activity of the soul in which it conceives that which it sees.

It should, however, be added that even the philosophers of antiquity (which here and elsewhere always means the philosophers of Greece and the Middle Ages) looked upon the active effort of discursive thought as the properly human element in our knowledge; it is the *ratio*, they held, which is distinctively human; the *intellectus* they regarded as being already beyond the sphere allotted to man. And yet it

---

[5] Fragment 112 (Diels).

belonged to man, though in one sense "superhuman"; the "purely human" by itself could not satiate man's powers of comprehension, for man, of his very nature, reaches out beyond the sphere of the "human", touching on the order of pure spirits. "Although the knowledge which is most characteristic of the human soul occurs in the mode of *ratio*, nevertheless there is in it a sort of participation in the simple knowledge which is proper to higher beings, of whom it is therefore said that they possess the faculty of spiritual vision." That is how the matter is put by Aquinas in the *Quaestiones disputate de veritate*.[6] It means to say that man participates in the angelic faculty of non-discursive vision, which is the capacity to apprehend the spiritual in the same manner that our eye apprehends light or our ear sound. Our knowledge in fact includes an element of non-activity, of purely receptive vision—though it is certainly not essentially human; it is, rather, the fulfillment of the highest promise in man, and thus, again, truly human (just as Aquinas calls the *vita contemplativa* "non proprie humana, sed superhumana",[7] not really human but superhuman, although it is the noblest mode of human life).

The philosophical tradition of antiquity did, therefore, recognize the element of work in man's mode of knowledge as specifically human. For the use of the *ratio*, discursive thought, requires real hard work.

The simple vision of the *intellectus*, however, contemplation, is *not* work. If, as this philosophical tradition holds, man's spiritual knowledge is the fruit of *ratio* and *intellectus*; if the discursive element is fused with "intellectual contemplation" and if, moreover, knowledge in philosophy, which

[6] *Quaest. disp. de veritate*, 15, 1.
[7] *Quaest. disp. de virtutibus cardinalibus*, 5, 1.

is directed upon the whole of being, is to preserve the element of contemplation, then it is not enough to describe this knowledge as work, for that would be to omit something essential. Knowledge in general, and more especially philosophical knowledge, is certainly quite impossible without work, without the *labor improbus* of discursive thought. Nevertheless there is also that about it which, essentially, is not work.

The statement that "knowledge is work"—because "knowing" is activity, pure activity—has two aspects: it expresses a claim *on* man and a claim *by* man. If you want to know something then you must work; in philosophy "the law is that reason acquires its possessions through work"[8] that is the claim on man. But there is another, a subtler claim, not perhaps immediately visible, in the statement, the claim made by man: if to know is to work, then knowledge is the fruit of our own unaided effort and activity; then knowledge includes nothing which is not due to the effort of man, and there is nothing *gratuitous* about it, nothing "inspired", nothing "given" about it.

To sum up: the essence of human cognition, on this view, is that it is exclusively an active, discursive labor of the *ratio*, the reason; and the notion "intellectual work" and "intellectual worker" acquires a quite special weight if we accept this point of view.

Look at the "worker" and you will see that his face is marked by strain and tension, and these are even more pronounced in the case of the "intellectual worker". These are the marks of that perpetual activity (exclusive of all else) of which Goethe remarked that "it ends in bankruptcy".[9] They are the revealing marks of the intellectual sclerosis that

[8] Kant, *loc. cit.*
[9] *Maximen und Reflexionen*, No. 1415 (edition Günther Müller, 1943).

comes with not being able to receive or accept, of that hardening of the heart that refuses to suffer anything; and in their extreme form such tensions become vocal in the lunatic assertion "every action has some meaning, even a crime; but to be passive is always senseless."[10]

Now discursive thought and intellectual contemplation are not simply related to one another as activity to receptivity, or as tense effort to passive acceptance. They are also related to one another as toil and trouble on the one hand and effortless possession on the other. And this antithesis—toil and trouble on one side, effortless ease on the other—is the occasion of yet another reason for the special stress on the notion of "intellectual work". So that we must now consider, for a moment, a particular view of the criterion of the worth and worthlessness of human behavior in general.

When Kant speaks of philosophizing as a "herculean labor",[11] he does not simply mean that it is characteristic of philosophizing; he regards the labor involved as a justification of philosophy: philosophizing is genuine in so far as it is "herculean labor". And it is because, as he contemptuously remarks, "intellectual contemplation" costs nobody anything that it is so very questionable. He expects nothing from "intellectual contemplation" *because* it costs nothing, and because contemplation is effortless. But that is surely on the way (if not even closer) to the view that the *effort* of acquiring knowledge gives one the assurance of the material *truth* of the knowledge acquired.

And there, in turn, we are not so very far from the ethical notion that everything man does naturally and without effort is a falsification of true morality—for what we do by nature is done without effort. In Kant's view, indeed, the fact that

---

[10] Hermann Rauschning, *Gespräche mit Hitler* (Zurich, 1940).

[11] Loc. cit., p. 390.

man's natural bent is contrary to the moral law, belongs to the concept of moral law. It is normal and essential, on this view, that the good should be difficult, and that the effort of will required in forcing oneself to perform some action should become the yardstick of the moral good: the more difficult a thing, the higher it is in the order of goodness. Schiller's ironical couplet hits off the weakness of this point of view:

> Gerne dient'ich den Freunden, doch tu ich es leider mit
>   Neigung,
> Und so wurmt es mir oft, dass ich nicht tugendhaft bin.[12]
> (How willingly I'd serve my friends, but alas, I do so
>   with pleasure,
> And so I am often worried by the fact that I am not virtuous.)

Hard work, then, is what is good. That is not by any means a new view, and it was put forward by Antisthenes the Cynic,[13] one of Plato's companions among those who grouped themselves round Socrates. Antisthenes is one of those surprisingly modern figures that occur here and there, and it is he who left us the first sketch of the "worker", or more accurately, perhaps, who represents that figure. Antisthenes is not only the author of the phrase just quoted about hard work; he is also responsible for making Hercules the human ideal, because he performed superhuman labors:[14] an ideal that has retained (or has it reacquired it?) a certain force from the days of Erasmus[15] and Kant—who labeled philo-

---

[12] Schiller, *Die Philosophen*.

[13] Found in Diogenes Laertius, *The Lives and Opinions of Renowned Philosophers*, VI, Book I, Cap. 2.

[14] Ibid. One of Antisthenes' works bears the title *The Greater Hercules, or Of Power*.

[15] Anton Gail has drawn my attention to the fact that in a portrait of Erasmus by Holbein (at Longford Castle) Erasmus' hands are resting on a book in which are to be read the words: "Herakleou ponoi—Erasmi Roterodami."

sophy with the heroic term "herculean"—down to those of Carlyle, the prophet of the religion of work:[16] You must work like Hercules. . . . Antisthenes the Cynic was a self-sufficient moralist, an autarchist, with no sense whatsoever of divine worship, even cracking Voltairian jokes about it;[17] he was insensible to the Muses and only liked poetry when it served to express moral truths;[18] and as for Eros, it evoked no reply in his heart: "Best of all", he remarked, "I would like to exterminate Aphrodite."[19] A dry realist, he did not, of course, believe in immortality; the one thing that matters is to live "an upright life" in this world.[20] It really looks as though all these traits had been gathered into one for the sake of providing an example in the abstract of the type "worker" pure and undefiled.

"Hard work is what is good"? In the *Summa Theologica* we find St. Thomas propounding a contrary opinion: "The essence of virtue consists in the good rather than in the difficult."[21] "Not everything that is more difficult is necessarily more meritorious; it must be more difficult in such a way that it is at the same time good in a yet higher way."[22] The Middle Ages also said something about virtue that is no longer so readily understood—least of all by Kant's compatriots and disciples—they held that virtue meant: "mastering our natural bent". No; that is what Kant would have said, and we all of us find it quite easy to understand; what Aquinas says is that virtue makes us perfect by enabling us to

---

[16] Carlyle, quoted by Robert Langewiesche.

[17] Cf. Wiehelm Nestle: *Griechische Geistesgeschichte von Homer bis Lukian*, 1944, pp. 313ff.

[18] Ibid., p. 314.

[19] Quoted by Clement of Alexandria.

[20] Cf. Diogenes Laertius, VI, 1.5.

[21] *Summa Theologica*, II-II, 123, 12 ad 2.

[22] Ibid., II-II, 27, 8 ad 2.

follow our natural bent in the right way.[23] In fact, he says, the sublime achievements of moral goodness are characterized by effortlessness—because it is of their essence to spring from love.

The tendency to overvalue hard work and the effort of doing something *difficult* is so deep-rooted that it even infects our notion of love. Why should it be that the average Christian regards loving one's enemy as the most exalted form of love? Principally because it offers an example of a natural bent heroically curbed; the exceptional difficulty, the impossibility one might almost say, of loving one's enemy constitutes the greatness of the love. And what does Aquinas say? "It is not the difficulty of loving one's enemy that matters when the essence of the merit of doing so is concerned, excepting in so far as the perfection of love wipes out the difficulty. And therefore, if love were to be so perfect that the difficulty vanished altogether—it would be more meritorious still."[24]

And in the same way, the essence of *knowledge* does not consist in the effort for which it calls, but in grasping existing things and in unveiling reality. Moreover, just as the highest form of virtue knows nothing of "difficulty", so too the highest form of knowledge comes to man like a gift— the sudden illumination, a stroke of genius, true contemplation; it comes effortlessly and without trouble. On one occasion St. Thomas speaks of contemplation and play in the same breath: "because of the leisure that goes with contemplation" the divine wisdom itself, Holy Scripture says, is "always at play, playing through the whole world" (Prov 8:30f.).[25]

[23] Ibid., II-II, 108, 2.
[24] *Quaest. disp. de caritate*, 8 ad 17.
[25] Commentary on Proverbs, 1, d. 2 (expositio tertius).

The highest forms of knowledge, on the other hand, may well be preceded by a great effort of thought, and perhaps this must be so (unless the knowledge in question were grace in the strict sense of the word); but in any case, the effort is not the cause; it is the condition. It is equally true that the effects so effortlessly produced by love presuppose no doubt a heroic moral struggle of the will. But the decisive thing is that virtue means the realization of the good; it may imply a previous moral effort, but it cannot be equated with moral effort. And similarly to know means to reach the reality of existing things; knowledge is not confined to effort of thought. It is more than "intellectual work".

This aspect too of "intellectual work"—the exaggerated value which is put upon the "difficult" simply because it is difficult—becomes evident in the accentuation of a particular trait in the look of the "worker": the fixed, mask-like readiness to suffer *in vacuo*, without relation to anything. It is the absence of any connection with reality or real values that is distinctive. And it is because this readiness to suffer (which has been called the heart of discipline, of whatever kind)[26] never asks the question "to what end" that it is utterly different from the Christian conception of sacrifice. The Christian conception of sacrifice is not concerned with the suffering involved *qua* suffering, it is not primarily concerned with the toil and the worry and with the difficulty, but with salvation, with the fullness of being, and thus ultimately with the fullness of happiness: "The end and the norm of discipline is happiness."[27]

The inmost significance of the exaggerated value which is set upon hard work appears to be this: man seems to mistrust

---

[26] Ernst Jünger, *Blätter und Steine*, p. 179.
[27] *Summa Theologica*, II-II, 141, 5 ad 1.

everything that is effortless; he can only enjoy, with a good conscience, what he has acquired with toil and trouble; he refuses to have anything as a gift.

We have only to think for a moment how much the Christian understanding of life depends upon the existence of "Grace"; let us recall that the Holy Spirit of God is himself called a "gift"[28] in a special sense; that the great teachers of Christianity say that the premise of God's justice is his love;[29] that everything gained and everything claimed follows upon something given, and comes after something gratuitous and unearned; that in the beginning there is always a gift—we have only to think of all this for a moment in order to see what a chasm separates the tradition of the Christian West and that other view.

In attempting to get to the source of the notion "intellectual work", we have seen that it can be traced in the main to two principal themes: the first is the view which regards human knowledge as exclusively attributable to discursive thought; the second is the contention that the effort which knowledge requires is a criterion of its truth. There is, however, a third element, more important than either of the foregoing, and which appears to involve both of them. It is the social implication of "intellectual work" that comes more fully to light in the expression "intellectual worker".

Work as it is understood in this phrase and context means the same thing as social service. "Intellectual work" in this context would mean intellectual activity in so far as it is a social service, in so far as it is a contribution to the common need. But that is not all that is implied by the words "intellectual work" and "intellectual worker". In the cur-

---

[28] *Summa contra Gentes*, 4, 23; cf. also *Summa Theologica*, I, 38, 2 ad 1.
[29] *Summa Theologica*, I, 21, 14.

rent usage of today what is further implied is respect for the "working class". What is really meant is roughly this: like the wage-earner, the manual worker and the proletarian, the educated man, the scholar, too, is a worker, in fact an "intellectual worker", and he, too, is harnessed to the social system and takes his place in the division of labor; he is allotted his place and his function among the workers; he is a functionary in the world of "total work"; he may be called a specialist, but he is a functionary. And that is what brings out the problem which really lies behind our question, in all its colors. That problem, it need hardly be said, is not just a theoretical one; it is the root problem with which we began our discussion: are we to build our house in the European tradition?

And yet the social aspect, as it concerns the relations of the strata of society and of its various groups, is only the foreground of the question; and to that we shall return. The real question is a metaphysical one. It is the old question of the rights and the meaning of the liberal arts. What are the liberal arts? In his commentary on Aristotle's *Metaphysics*, Aquinas gives this definition: "Only those arts are called liberal or free which are concerned with knowledge; those which are concerned with utilitarian ends that are attained through activity, however, are called servile."[30] "I know well", Newman says, "that knowledge may resolve itself into an art, and seminate in a mechanical process and in tangible fruit; but it may also fall back upon that Reason, which informs it, and resolve itself into Philosophy. For in one case it is called Useful Knowledge, in the other Liberal."[31] The liberal arts, then, include all forms of human activity which

[30] Commentary on the *Metaphysics*, I, 3.
[31] John Henry Cardinal Newman: *Idea of a University*, V, 6.

are an end in themselves; the servile arts are those which
have an end beyond themselves, and more precisely an end
which consists in a utilitarian result attainable in practice, a
practicable result.

Put in this form the question will seem to many people an
anachronism, and the very terms "liberal arts" and "servile
arts" sound antiquated and meaningless. But translated into
the terminology of the present day the question means precisely this: Is there a sphere of human activity, one might
even say of human existence, that does not need to be justi-
fied by inclusion in a five-year plan and its technical organization? Is there such a thing, or not? The inner meaning of
the concepts "intellectual work" and "intellectual worker"
points to the answer "No." Man, from this point of view,
is essentially a functionary, an official, even in the highest
reaches of his activity.

Let us examine the question in terms of philosophy and
philosophical education. For philosophy can be regarded as
the freest of the liberal arts.[32] "Knowledge is most truly free
when it is philosophical knowledge", says Cardinal Newman.[33] In a sense, too, philosophy has become the symbol
for all the *artes liberales*; in German universities the "Faculty
of Arts" of the medieval university is nowadays called the
"Philosophical Faculty".

Philosophy and its status, then, offers a valuable lead to
the direction in which the answer to the question lies.

There can be no serious disagreement on the role of the
natural sciences, of medicine, law, and economics in modern
society. Within the functional nexus of the modern body social, characterized as it is by division of labor, these sciences

[32] This question is treated at greater length on pp. 87ff.
[33] Newman, ibid.

have their clearly defined place. They therefore come under the heading of work in the social sense, which we are discussing. It is in the nature of the sciences to be applicable to ends outside themselves. But there are also the "pure" sciences practiced in a philosophical manner, and to them our question applies in the same way as it does to philosophy itself. When we say of a science that it is practiced in a "philosophical manner", we mean it is undertaken "academically" in the original sense of the word (for "academic" means "philosophical" or it means nothing at all).

When, therefore, we discuss the place and justification of philosophy we are discussing no more nor less than the place and justification of the university, of academic education itself in the true sense—that is, the sense in which it differs fundamentally from mere professional training and goes beyond such training in principle. A functionary is trained. Training is defined as being concerned with some one side or aspect of man, with regard to some special subject. Education concerns the whole man; an educated man is a man with a point of view from which he takes in the whole world. Education concerns the whole man, man *capax universi*, capable of grasping the totality of existing things.

This implies nothing against training and nothing against the official. Of course specialized and professional work is *normal, the* normal way in which men play their part in the world; "work" is the normal, the working day is the ordinary day. But the question is: whether the world, defined as the world of work, is exhaustively defined; can man develop to the full as a functionary and a "worker" and nothing else; can a full human existence be contained within an exclusively workaday existence? Stated differently and translated back into our terms: is there such a thing as a liberal art? The doctrinaire planners of the world of "total work" must answer "No." The worker's world, as Ernst Jünger puts it, is "the denial of free scholarship and inquiry."[34] In a consistently planned "worker" State there is no room for philosophy because philosophy cannot serve other ends than its own or it ceases to be philosophy; nor can the sciences be carried on in a philosophical manner, which means to say that there can be no such thing as university (academic) education in the full sense of the word. And it is above all the expression "intellectual worker" that epigrammatically confirms the fact that this is impossible. And that is why it is so alarmingly symptomatic that ordinary usage, and even university custom, allows the term "intellectual worker" and sometimes permits "brain worker".

The ancients, however, maintained that there was a legitimate place for non-utilitarian modes of human activity, in other words, liberal arts. The knowledge of the functionary is not the only knowledge; there is also "the knowledge of a gentleman" (to use Newman's very happy formula in the *Idea of a University*, for the term *artes liberales*).

There is no need to waste words showing that not everything is useless which cannot be brought under the definition of the useful. And it is by no means unimportant for a nation and for the realization of the "common good", that a place should be made for activity which is not "useful work" in the sense of being utilitarian. "I have never bothered or asked", Goethe said to Friedrich Soret in 1830, "in what way I was useful to society as a whole; I contented myself with expressing what I recognized as good and true. That has certainly been useful in a wide circle; but that was not the aim; it was the necessary result."[35]

[34] *Blätter und Steine*, p. 176.
[35] Quoted in [Johann Peter] Eckermann's *Conversations*.

In the Middle Ages the same view prevailed. "It is necessary for the perfection of human society", Aquinas writes, "that there should be men who devote their lives to contemplation"[36] —*nota bene*, necessary not only for the good of the individual who so devotes himself, but for the good of human society. No one thinking in terms of "intellectual worker" could have said that.

[36] Commentary on Proverbs.

III

The "worker", it has been seen in our brief analysis of that significant figure, is characterized by three principal traits: an extreme tension of the powers of action, a readiness to suffer *in vacuo* unrelated to anything, and complete absorption in the social organism, itself rationally planned to utilitarian ends. Leisure, from this point of view, appears as something wholly fortuitous and strange, without rhyme or reason, and, morally speaking, unseemly: another word for laziness, idleness and sloth. At the zenith of the Middle Ages, on the contrary, it was held that sloth and restlessness, "leisurelessness", the incapacity to enjoy leisure, were all closely connected; sloth was held to be the source of restlessness, and the ultimate cause of "work for work's sake". It may well seem paradoxical to maintain that the restlessness at the bottom of a fanatical and suicidal activity should come from the lack of will to action; a surprising thought, that we shall only be able to decipher with effort. But it is a worthwhile effort, and we should do well to pause for a moment to inquire into the philosophy of life attached to the word *acedia*.[1] In the first place *acedia* does not signify the "idleness" we envisage when we speak of idleness as "the root of all vice". Idleness, in the medieval view, means that a man renounces the claim implicit in his human dignity.

[1] See Josef Pieper, *Über die Hoffnung*, p. 55. *Faith, Hope, and Love* (San Francisco: Ignatius Press 1997), pp. 117 ff.

In a word, he does not want to be as God wants him to
be, and that ultimately means that he does not wish to be
what he really, fundamentally, *is*. *Acedia* is the "despair from
weakness" which Kierkegaard analyzed as the "despairing
refusal to be oneself".[2] Metaphysically and theologically,
the notion of *acedia* means that a man does not, in the last
resort, give the consent of his will to his own being; that
beneath the dynamic activity of his existence, he is still not
at one with himself; that, as the Middle Ages expressed it,
sadness overwhelms him when he is confronted with the
divine goodness immanent in himself (that sadness which is
the *tristitia saeculi* of Holy Scripture).[3]

And then we are told that the opposite of this metaphysical
and theological notion is the notion "hardworking", industrious, in the context of economic life! For *acedia* has, in fact,
been interpreted as though it had something to do with the
economic ethos of the Middle Ages. Sombart, for example,
treats it as though it were the fault of the lazy stay-at-home
as compared with the industrious worker[4]—though Max
Scheler criticized his view.[5] And some of Sombart's succes-
sors even go so far as to translate *acedia* as "stick-in-the-mud"
—as well say "lack of business enterprise" or even "lack of
salesmanship".[6] All this, however, is less painful than the
eager attempt of the apologist to make Christian teaching
square with a passing fashion, which in this case involves
interpreting the Church's view of work in terms of modern activism—with the result that *vivere secundum actum est*

[2] *Sickness unto Death*, pp. 74ff.
[3] *Quaest. disp. de malo*, 11, 3.
[4] W. Sombart, *Der Bourgeois*, pp. 322, 313, 321 (1913).
[5] Max Scheler, *Vom Umsturz der Werte*, Vol. II, p. 293 (1919).
[6] Johannes Haessle, *Das Arbeitsethos der Kirche nach Thomas von Aquin und Leo XIII*, p. 31 (1923).

quando exercet quis opera vitae in actu[7] is actually translated as
"life in actu consists in this, that one is busy and occupied
with practical affairs"[8] . . . as if Aquinas did not hold that
contemplation was an *opus vitae*!

No, the contrary of *acedia* is not the spirit of work in the
sense of the work of every day, of earning one's living; it
is man's happy and cheerful affirmation of his own being,
his acquiescence in the world and in God—which is to say
love. Love that certainly brings a particular freshness and
readiness to work along with it, but that no one with the
least experience could conceivably confuse with the tense
activity of the fanatical "worker".

Who would guess, unless he were expressly told so, that
Aquinas regarded *acedia* as a sin against the third commandment? He was in fact so far from considering idleness as the
opposite of the ethos of work that he simply interprets it as
an offense against the commandment in which we are called
upon to have "the peace of the mind in God".[9]

But what has all this, one might well ask, to do with
the question? *Acedia* was reckoned among the *vitia capitalia*,
as one of the seven capital or cardinal sins, for they were
not called "capital" because of the best-known rendering
of *caput*; *caput* certainly means "head", but it also means
"source" or "spring"—and that is the meaning in this case.
They are sins from which other faults follow "naturally",
one is tempted to say, as from a source. Idleness—and this
is how we get back to the question—idleness, according to
traditional teaching, is the source of many faults and among
others of that deep-seated lack of calm which makes leisure
impossible. Among other faults, certainly, and one of the

[7] *De unitate intellectus.*
[8] Johannes Haessle, loc. cit.
[9] *Summa Theologica*, II-II, 35, 3 ad 1; *Quaest. disp. de malo*, 11, 3 ad 2.

children of *acedia*, is despair, which amounts to saying that despair and the incapacity for leisure are twins—a revealing thought that explains, among other things, the hidden meaning of that very questionable saying, "work and don't despair."

Idleness, in the old sense of the word, so far from being synonymous with leisure, is more nearly the inner prerequisite which renders leisure impossible: it might be described as the utter absence of leisure, or the very opposite of leisure. Leisure is only possible when a man is at one with himself, when he acquiesces in his own being, whereas the essence of *acedia* is the refusal to acquiesce in one's own being. Idleness and the incapacity for leisure correspond with one another. Leisure is the contrary of both.

Leisure, it must be clearly understood, is a mental and spiritual attitude—it is not simply the result of external factors, it is not the inevitable result of spare time, a holiday, a weekend or a vacation. It is, in the first place, an attitude of mind, a condition of the soul, and as such utterly contrary to the ideal of "worker" in each and every one of the three aspects under which it was analyzed: work as activity, as toil, as a social function.

Compared with the exclusive ideal of work as activity, leisure implies (in the first place) an attitude of non-activity, of inward calm, of silence; it means not being "busy", but letting things happen.

Leisure is a form of silence, of that silence which is the prerequisite of the apprehension of reality: only the silent hear and those who do not remain silent do not hear. Silence, as it is used in this context, does not mean "dumbness" or "noiselessness"; it means more nearly that the soul's power to "answer" to the reality of the world is left undisturbed. For leisure is a receptive attitude of mind, a contemplative attitude, and it is not only the occasion but also the capacity for steeping oneself in the whole of creation.

Furthermore, there is also a certain serenity in leisure. That serenity springs precisely from our inability to understand, from our recognition of the mysterious nature of the universe; it springs from the courage of deep confidence, so that we are content to let things take their course; and there is something about it which Konrad Weiss, the poet, called "confidence in the fragmentariness of life and history." In the same entry in his Journal he refers to the characteristically precise style and thought of Ernst Jünger, with his fanaticism for the truth[10]—Jünger, who really seems to tear the mystery out of a thing, coldly and boldly, and then lay it out, neatly dissected, all ready to view. His passion for tidy formulae "is surely the very reverse of contemplative, and yet there is something idle in it, idleness concealed within the sublime exactitude of thought—as opposed to the true idleness which lets God and the world and things go, and gives them time . . . !

Leisure is not the attitude of mind of those who actively intervene, but of those who are open to everything; not of those who grab and grab hold, but of those who leave the reins loose and who are free and easy themselves—almost like a man falling asleep, for one can only fall asleep by "letting oneself go". Sleeplessness and the incapacity for leisure are really related to one another in a special sense, and a man at leisure is not unlike a man asleep. Heraclitus the Obscure observed of men who were asleep that they too "were busy and active in the happenings of the world."[11] When we really let our minds rest contemplatively on a rose in bud,

[10] In the entry dated Sept. 12, 1939.
[11] Fragment 75 (Diels).

on a child at play, on a divine mystery, we are rested and quickened as though by a dreamless sleep. Or as the Book of Job says, "God giveth songs in the night" (Job 35:10). Moreover, it has always been a pious belief that God sends his good gifts and his blessings in sleep. And in the same way his great, imperishable intuitions visit a man in his moments of leisure. It is in these silent and receptive moments that the soul of man is sometimes visited by an awareness of what holds the world together:

> was die Welt
> Im innersten zusammenhält

only for a moment perhaps, and the lightning vision of his intuition has to be recaptured and rediscovered in hard work.

Compared with the exclusive ideal of work as toil, leisure appears (*secondly*) in its character as an attitude of contemplative "celebration", a word that, properly understood, goes to the very heart of what we mean by leisure. Leisure is possible only on the premise that man consents to his own true nature and abides in concord with the meaning of the universe (whereas idleness, as we have said, is the refusal of such consent). Leisure draws its vitality from affirmation. It is not the same as non-activity, nor is it identical with tranquility; it is not even the same as inward tranquility. Rather, it is like the tranquil silence of lovers, which draws its strength from concord.

In his fragment *Leisure* Hölderlin writes:

> I stand in the peaceful mowing
> Like a loving elm tree, while sweetly life plays
> And twines around me like vines and clusters of grapes.

And we may read in the first chapter of Genesis that God "ended his work which he had made" and "behold, it was very good." In leisure, man too celebrates the end of his work by allowing his inner eye to dwell for a while upon the reality of the Creation. He looks and he affirms: it is good.

Now the highest form of affirmation is the festival; among its characteristics, Karl Kerényi tells us, is "the union of tranquility, contemplation, and intensity of life."[12] To hold a celebration means to affirm the basic meaningfulness of the universe and a sense of oneness with it, of inclusion within it. In celebrating, in holding festivals upon occasion, man experiences the world in an aspect other than the everyday one.

The festival is the origin of leisure, and the inward and ever-present meaning of leisure. And because leisure is thus by its nature a celebration, it is more than effortless; it is the direct opposite of effort.

And *thirdly*, leisure stands opposed to the exclusive ideal of work *qua* social function. A break in one's work, whether of an hour, a day or a week, is still part of the world of work. It is a link in the chain of utilitarian functions. The pause is made for the sake of work and in order to work, and a man is not only refreshed *from* work but *for* work. Leisure is an altogether different matter; it is no longer on the same plane; it runs at right angles to work—just as it could be said that intuition is not the prolongation or continuation, as it were, of the work of the *ratio*, but cuts right across it, vertically. *Ratio*, in point of fact, used to be compared to time, whereas *intellectus* was compared to eternity, to the eternal now.[13] And therefore leisure does not exist for the sake of work—however much strength it may give a man to

---

[12] Karl Kerényi, *Die antike Religion*, p. 66 (1940).
[13] *Summa contra Gentes*, II, 96.

work; the point of leisure is not to be a restorative, a pick-me-up, whether mental or physical; and though it gives new strength, mentally and physically, and spiritually too, that is not the point.

Leisure, like contemplation, is of a higher order than the *vita activa* (although the active life is the proper human life in a more special sense). And order, in this sense, cannot be overturned or reversed. Thus, however true it may be that the man who says his nightly prayers sleeps the better for it, nevertheless no one could say his nightly prayers with that in mind. In the same way, no one who looks to leisure simply to restore his working powers will ever discover the fruit of leisure; he will never know the quickening that follows, almost as though from some deep sleep.

The point and the justification of leisure are not that the functionary should function faultlessly and without a breakdown, but that the functionary should continue to be a man —and that means that he should not be wholly absorbed in the clear-cut milieu of his strictly limited function; the point is also that he should retain the faculty of grasping the world as a whole and realizing his full potentialities as an entity meant to reach Wholeness.[14]

Because Wholeness is what man strives for, the power to achieve leisure is one of the fundamental powers of the human soul. Like the gift for contemplative absorption in the things that are, and like the capacity of the spirit to soar in festive celebration, the power to know leisure is the power

[14] "As God, who made all things, did not rest *in* those things . . . but rested *in* himself *from* the created works . . . so we too should learn not to regard the works as the goal, but to rest *from* the works in God himself, in whom our felicity lies. That is the reason that man is supposed to work for six days on his own works, but on the seventh day to rest and be free for the worship of God. But this resting has been pledged to the Christian not for a time, but for ever." Aquinas, Commentary on the *Sentences*, 2d. 15, 3, 3.

to overstep the boundaries of the workaday world and reach out to superhuman, life-giving existential forces that refresh and renew us before we turn back to our daily work. Only in genuine leisure does a "gate to freedom" open. Through that gate man may escape from the "restricted area" of that "latent anxiety" which a keen observer has perceived to be the mark of the world of work, where "work and unemployment are the two inescapable poles of existence."[15]

In leisure—not of course exclusively in leisure, but always in leisure—the truly human values are saved and preserved *because* leisure is the means whereby the sphere of the "specifically human" can, over and again, be left behind—not as a result of any violent effort to reach out, but as in an ecstasy (the ecstasy is indeed more "difficult" than the most violent exertion, more "difficult" because not invariably at our beck and call; a state of extreme tension is more easily induced than a state of relaxation and ease *although* the latter is effortless); the full enjoyment of leisure is hedged in by paradoxes of this kind, and it is itself a state at once very human and superhuman. Aristotle says of leisure, "A man will live thus, not to the extent that he is a man, but to the extent that a divine principle dwells within him."[16]

---

[15] Richard Wright in *Die Umschau*, Vol. I, Heft 2, pp. 214–16.
[16] *Nicomachean Ethics*, 10, 7 (1177b).

IV

In the foregoing sections leisure was tentatively defined and outlined in its ideal form. It now remains to consider the problem of realizing its "hopes", of its latent powers of gaining acceptance, and its possible impetus in history. The practical problem involved might be stated thus: Is it possible, from now on, to maintain and defend, or even to reconquer, the right and claims of leisure, in face of the claims of "total labor" that are invading every sphere of life? Leisure, it must be remembered, is not a Sunday afternoon idyll, but the preserve of freedom, of education and culture, and of that undiminished humanity which views the world as a whole. In other words, is it going to be possible to save men from becoming officials and functionaries and "workers" to the exclusion of all else? Can that possibly be done, and if so in what circumstances? There is no doubt of one thing: the world of the "worker" is taking shape with dynamic force—with such a velocity that, rightly or wrongly, one is tempted to speak of demonic force in history.

The attempt to withstand this invasion has been made at a number of different points for some time past. It is even possible to lay down that certain forms of opposition are inadequate; for example the position—quite legitimate up to a point—called "art for art's sake", was an attempt to isolate the realm of art from the universal utilitarianism that seeks to turn everything in the world to some useful purpose. In our own day the real historical fronts still remain to some extent fluid, masked by backward-looking interim solutions. Among these are the return to "tradition" pure and simple; an emphasis on our duty as the heirs of classical antiquity; the struggle to retain the classics in the schools and the "academic" (philosophical) character of the universities—in a word *humanism*. Such are the designations of some of the positions from which a threatened and endangered body aspires to defend itself.

The question is whether these positions will be held and in fact whether they *can* be held. The problem is whether "Humanism" is an adequate watchword—adequate, not simply as a psychologically good rallying cry, as an effective summons to battle, but as a conception metaphysically sound and therefore ultimately credible, in the sense of providing a genuine source of power capable of influencing the course of history. ("Humanism", it should here be observed, has recently made its appearance in Eastern Germany, where it has become the fashion to speak of economic materialism as "humanistic"; and in France, an atheistic existentialism also claims to be humanistic—neither usage, what is more, is entirely without justification!) The real question is therefore, whether an appeal to "humanism" is adequate—in face of the totalitarian claims of the world of work.

Before we attempt an answer to this question, we must clear away a number of obvious misunderstandings, which have no doubt already arisen, by saying something about the social aspect of our problem. This is the reason for our excursus on the proletariat and deproletarianization.

Excursus on the Proletariat and Deproletarianization

It has already been explained that the term "intellectual worker" adds pointed expression to the claims of the world of work. But a modern German dictionary (Trübner's) maintains, on the contrary, that the relatively modern terms "intellectual work", "intellectual worker" are valuable because "they do away with the age-old distinction, still further emphasized in modern times, between the manual worker and the educated man."[1] Now, if that designation is *not* accepted, or at least only with reservations, it surely implies a certain conception of those social contrasts? The refusal to allow the validity of the term "intellectual worker" certainly means one thing: it means that the common denominator "work" and "worker" is not considered a proper or a possible basis upon which to bridge the contrast of the classes of society. But does it not mean something more? Does it not mean that the gulf between an educated class which is free to pursue knowledge as an end in itself, and the proletarian who knows nothing beyond the spare time which is barely sufficient for him to renew his strength for his daily work —does it not mean logically, from our point of view, that this gulf is in fact necessarily deepened and widened, independently of whatever subjective views and intentions may be at work? This objection is not to be taken lightly.

Indeed, on one occasion Plato contrasts the figure of the philosopher with that of the *bánausos*, the common working man. Philosophers are those

> who have not grown up like serfs, but in quite different, not to say contrary, circumstances. Now this, O Theodorus, is the way of each one individually: the one whom you call a philosopher, is truly brought up in freedom and leisure, and goes unpunished though he seems simple and useless when it is a matter of menial offices, even though he should not, for instance, know how to tie up a parcel that has to be sent on, or how to prepare a tasty dish . . . ; the other way is the way of those who know, indeed, how to perform

[1] Trübner's *Deutsches Wörterbuch* (Berlin, 1939).

> all these things well and smartly, but on the other hand do
> not even know how to wear their cloak like a gentleman,
> and still less how to prize the good life of gods and men in
> harmonious phrases.

This passage is to be found in Plato's *Theaetetus*.[2] It is to be
noted that the Greek conception of the *bánausos* (the common working man)—as might easily be shown from the
above quotation from Plato, means not only an uneducated
man, a man insensitive to poetry and art, and with no spiritual view of the world, but furthermore a man who lives
by manual labor as distinguished from the man who owns
sufficient property to dispose freely of his time. Here, once
again, does it not appear as though our thesis implied a return
to the Greek notion of the common working man and to
the social and educational conceptions of the pre-Christian
era? Certainly not! Yet is this not implicit in the refusal to
accept the term "work" (which, as has always been said, is
supposed to be a term of praise) as applying to the *whole*
sphere of man's intellectual and spiritual activity? On the
contrary, in my opinion everything must be done, on the
one hand to obliterate a contrast of this kind between the
classes, but on the other hand it is quite wrong, and indeed
foolish, to attempt to achieve that aim by looking for social unity in what is (for the moment!) the purely termi-
nological reduction of the educated stratum to proletarian
level, instead of the real abolition of the proletariat. What
do we mean, fundamentally, by the words "proletariat", and
"deproletarianization"?—It will be as well, in attempting to
answer the question and to define the terms, to leave firmly
aside all discussion of the practicability of "deproletarianizing", in order to answer the question purely "theoretically"
and from the point of view of the principles involved.

[2] *Theaetetus*, 175f.

In the first place, a proletarian and a poor man are not the same. A man may be poor without being a proletarian: a beggar in medieval society was certainly not a proletarian. Equally, a proletarian is not necessarily poor: a mechanic, a "specialist" or a "technician" in a "totalitarian work state" is certainly a proletarian. Secondly, this, though obvious, has to be said: the negative aspect of the notion "proletariat", the thing to be got rid of, does not consist in the fact that it is a condition limited to a particular stratum of society; so that the negative aspect would disappear once *all* had become proletarians. "Proletarianism" cannot obviously be overcome by making everyone proletarian.

What, then, is proletarianism? If the numerous sociological definitions and terms are reduced to a common denominator, the result might be expressed in the following terms: the proletarian is the man who is fettered to the process of work.

This still leaves the phrase "process of work" vague and in need of clarification. It does not, of course, mean work in the ordinary sense: the never-ceasing activity of man. "Process of work", here, means useful work in the sense already defined, of contributing to the general need, to the *bonum utile*. And so "process of work" means the all-embracing process in which things are used for the sake of the public need. To be fettered to work means to be bound to this vast utilitarian process in which our needs are satisfied, and, what is more, tied to such an extent that the life of the working man is wholly consumed in it.

To be tied in this way may be the result of various causes. The cause may be lack of property: everyone who is a propertyless wage-earner is a proletarian, everyone "who owns nothing but his power to work",[3] and who is consequently

---

[3] Pius XI, Encyclical *Quadragesimo anno*.

compelled to sell his capacity to work, is a proletarian. But to be tied to work may also be caused by coercion in a totalitarian state; in such a state everyone, whether propertied or unpropertied, is a proletarian because he is bound by the orders of others "to the necessities of an absolute economic process of production",[4] by outside forces, which means that he is entirely subject to economic forces, is a proletarian.

In the third place, to be tied to the process of work may be ultimately due to the inner impoverishment of the individual: in this context everyone whose life is completely filled by his work (in the special sense of the word work) is a proletarian because his life has shrunk inwardly, and contracted, with the result that he can no longer act significantly outside his work, and perhaps can no longer even conceive of such a thing.

Finally, all these different forms of proletarianism, particularly the last two, mutually attract one another and in so doing intensify each other. The "total work" State needs the spiritually impoverished, one-track mind of the "functionary"; and he, in his turn, is naturally inclined to find complete satisfaction in his "service" and thereby achieves the illusion of a life fulfilled, which he acknowledges and willingly accepts.

This inner constraint, the inner chains which fetter us to "work", prompts a further question: "proletarianism" thus understood, is perhaps a symptomatic state of mind common to *all* levels of society and by no means confined to the "proletariat", to the "worker", a *general* symptom that is merely found isolated in unusually acute form in the proletariat; so that it might be asked whether we are not all of

[4] Ibid.

us proletarians and all of us, consequently, ripe and ready to fall into the hands of some collective labor State and be at its disposal as functionaries—even though explicitly of the contrary political opinion. In that case, spiritual immunization against the seductive appeal and the power of totalitarian forms must, surely, be sought and hoped for at a much deeper level of thought than on the level of purely political considerations?[5]

In this context the distinction between the liberal and the servile arts acquires a fresh significance. In antiquity and the Middle Ages, the essence of the *artes serviles* was held to consist in their being directed, as St. Thomas says, "to the satisfaction of a need through activity." "Proletarianism" would then mean the limitation of existence and activity to the sphere of the *artes serviles*—whether this limitation were occasioned by lack of property, State compulsion, or spiritual impoverishment. By the same token, "deproletarianizing" would mean: enlarging the scope of life beyond the confines of merely useful servile work, and widening the sphere of servile work to the advantage of the liberal arts; and this process, once again, can only be carried out by combining three things: by giving the wage-earner the opportunity to save and acquire property, by limiting the power of the state, and by overcoming the inner impoverishment of the individual.

The phrase "servile work" strikes contemporary ears as extremely offensive—that is well known. Nevertheless, it

[5] Although in writing *Thesen zur sozialen Politik* (first published in 1933), I *expressly* limited myself to the consideration of political questions, and was therefore aware of the limitations of a purely political view, I now regard the essay as requiring completion at many points. It is surely characteristic of the generation formed between the wars that they expected in general too much from unadulterated politics.

would be a dangerous procedure to attempt to deny the "servility" of work. By setting up the fiction that work does *not* "serve" primarily for some purpose outside itself, we accomplish precisely the opposite of what we intended or pretended to accomplish. By no means do we "liberate" or "rehabilitate" the laboring man. Instead, we establish precisely that inhuman state characteristic of labor under totalitarianism: the ultimate tying of the worker to production. For the process of production itself is understood and proclaimed as the activity that gives meaning to human existence.

Genuine deproletarianization, which must not be confounded with the struggle against poverty (there is no need to waste words on the vital importance of *that*), assumes that the distinction between the *artes liberales* and the *artes serviles* is a meaningful one, that is, it must be recognized that there is a real distinction between useful activity on the one hand, the sense and purpose of which is not in itself, and on the other hand the liberal arts which cannot be put at the disposal of useful ends. And it is entirely consistent that those who stand for the "proletarianizing" of everyone, should deny all meaning to the distinction and try to prove that it has no basis in reality.

To take an example: the distinction between the liberal arts and the servile arts runs parallel with the terms: honorarium and wage. Properly speaking, the liberal arts receive an honorarium, while servile work receives a wage. The concept of honorarium implies that an incommensurability exists between performance and recompense, and that the performance cannot "really" be recompensed. Wages, on the other hand (in the extreme sense in which they differ from an honorarium), are intended as payment for the specific work performed, without consideration of the needs of the worker. It is significant that those members of the intelligentsia who are imbued with "working-class" ideals refuse to recognize this distinction between honorarium and wages. To their minds, only wages exist. In a sort of manifesto on the situation of the writer in society today,[6] in which literature is proclaimed a "social function", Jean-Paul Sartre announces that the writer, who has in the past so seldom "established a relation between his work and its material recompense", must learn to regard himself as "a worker who receives the reward of his effort." There, the incommensurability between the achievement and the reward, as it is implied and expressed in an "honorarium", is declared nonexistent even in the field of philosophy and poetry which are, on the contrary, simply "intellectual work". By contrast a social doctrine steeped in the tradition of Christian Europe would not only hold firmly to the distinction between an honorarium and a wage, it would not only hesitate to regard every reward as a wage; it would go further and would even maintain that there is no such thing as a recompense for a thing done which did not retain in some degree the character (whether much or little) of an honorarium, for even "servile" work cannot be entirely equated with the material recompense because it is a "human" action, so that it always retains something incommensurable with the recompense—just like the liberal arts.

And so it comes about, paradoxical though it may seem, that the proletarian dictator Stalin should say: "The worker must be paid according to the work done and not according to his needs",[7] and that the encyclical *Quadragesimo anno* which has for one of its principal aims the "deproletarianizing" of the masses, should assert that "in the first place the worker has the right to a wage sufficient to support himself

---

[6] Published in the first number of *Les Temps Modernes*.

[7] Joseph Stalin in a public statement made in 1933.

and his family."[8] On the one hand, there is an attempt to restrict and even to extirpate the liberal arts: it is alleged that only useful, "paying" work makes sense; on the other hand, there is an attempt to extend the character of "liberal art" deep down into every human action, even the humblest servile work. The former aims at making all men into proletarians, the latter at "deproletarianizing" the masses.

There is, however, a fact which from the vantage-point we have now reached must be strikingly clear and significant, and it is this: whereas the "total work" State declares all un-useful work "undesirable", and even expropriates free time in the service of work, there is one Institution in the world which forbids useful activity, and servile work, on particular days, and in this way prepares, as it were, a sphere for a non-proletarian existence.

Thus one of the first socialists, P. J. Proudhon (whom Marx dismissed as a "petit bourgeois")[9] was not so far wrong in beginning his work with a pamphlet on the celebration of Sunday, the social significance of which he expresses in the following words: "On one day in the week servants regained the dignity of human beings, and stood again on a level with their masters."[10] And in the introduction to his little book, Proudhon gets very near to the heart of the matter when he says, "Discussion about work and wages, organization and industry, which is so rife at present ought, it seems to me, to start with the study of a law which would have as its basis a theory of rest."[11] It is true that the full

[8] *Quadragesimo anno,* 55ff.

[9] P. J. Proudhon, *Die Sonntagsfeier, aus dem Gesichtspunkt des öffentlichen Gesundheitswesens, der Moral, der Familien- und bürgerlichen Verhältnisse betrachtet* (Kassel, 1850).

[10] Ibid., p. 18.

[11] Ibid., p. vi.

meaning of this "theory of rest" is not open to one who, like Proudhon, examines it exclusively "from the point of view of public health, morality, the family and social conditions." And here is something to be examined more closely.

Let us begin by summing up what has already been said in this excursus: If the essence of "proletarian" is the fact of being fettered to the process of work, then the central problem of liberating men from this condition lies in making a whole field of significant activity available and open to the working man—of activity which is *not* "work"; in other words: in making the sphere of real leisure available to him.

This end cannot be attained by purely political measures and by widening and, in that sense, "freeing" the life of the individual economically. Although this would entail much that is necessary, the essential would still be wanting. The provision of an external opportunity for leisure is not enough; it can only be fruitful if the man himself is capable of leisure and can, as we say, "occupy his leisure", or (as the Greeks still more clearly say) *skolen agein*, "work his leisure" (this usage brings out very clearly the by no means "leisurely" character of leisure).

"That is the principal point: with what kind of activity is man to occupy his leisure"[12]—who would suspect that that was a sentence taken from a book more than two thousand years old, none other than the *Politics* of Aristotle? What, then, ultimately makes leisure inwardly possible and, at the same time, what is its real justification?

---

[12] Aristotle, *Politics*, 8, 3 (1337b).

V

What, then, ultimately makes leisure inwardly possible and, at the same time, what is its fundamental justification?

In posing this question we are asking again: Can the realm of leisure be saved and its foundations upheld by an appeal to *humanism?* On closer inspection it will be seen that "humanism", understood as a mere appeal to a *humanum*, does not serve.

The soul of leisure, it can be said, lies in "celebration". Celebration is the point at which the three elements of leisure come to a focus: relaxation, effortlessness, and superiority of "active leisure" to all functions.

But if celebration is the core of leisure, then leisure can only be made possible and justifiable on the same basis as the celebration of a festival. *That basis is divine worship.*

The meaning of celebration, we have said, is man's affirmation of the universe and his experiencing the world in an aspect other than its everyday one. Now we cannot conceive a more intense affirmation of the world than "praise of God", praise of the Creator of this very world. This statement is generally received with a discomfort formed of many elements—I have often witnessed that. But its truth is irrefutable. The most festive festival it is possible to celebrate is divine worship. And there is no festival that does not draw its vitality from worship and that has not become a festival by virtue of its origin in worship. There is no such thing as a festival "without gods"—whether it be a carnival or a marriage. That is not a demand, or a requirement; it does not mean that that is how things ought to be. Rather, it is meant as a simple statement of fact: however dim the recollection of the association may have become in men's minds, a feast "without gods", and unrelated to worship, is quite simply unknown. It is true that ever since the French Revolution attempts have repeatedly been made to manufacture feast days and holidays that have no connection with divine worship, or are sometimes even opposed to it: "Brutus days", or even that hybrid, "Labor Day". In point of fact the stress and strain of giving them some kind of festal appearance is one of the very best proofs of the significance of divine worship for a feast; and nothing illustrates so clearly that festivity is only possible where divine worship is still a vital act—and nothing shows this so clearly as a comparison between a living and deeply traditional feast day, with its roots in divine worship, and one of those rootless celebrations, carefully and unspontaneously prepared beforehand, and as artificial as a maypole.

Certainly we must ask whether the great epoch of artificial festivals is not still to come. Perhaps we should be preparing ourselves for it. Might we not expect the forces of society or, in the extreme case, the holders of political power to lavish tremendous effort on specious arrangements for the sake of artificially engendering a sham festivity—an illusory, semi-opaque semblance of "holidays" that would be devoid of the true and ultimate affirmation of the world that is the essence of the festive. Such holidays, moreover, are in fact based on suppression of such affirmation; they derive their dangerous seductiveness precisely from that.

What is true of celebration is true of leisure: its possibility, its ultimate justification derive from its roots in divine worship. That is not a conceptual abstraction, but the simple truth as may be seen from the history of religion. What does a "day of rest" mean in the Bible, and for that matter in Greece and Rome? To rest from work means that time is reserved for divine worship: certain days and times are set aside and transferred to "the exclusive property of the gods."[1]

Divine worship means the same thing where time is concerned, as the temple where space is concerned. "Temple" means (as may be seen from the original sense of the word): that a particular piece of ground is specially reserved, and marked off from the remainder of the land which is used either for agriculture or for habitation. And this plot of land is transferred to the estate of the gods, it is neither lived on, nor cultivated. And similarly in divine worship a certain definite space of *time* is set aside from working hours and days, a limited time, specially marked off—and like the space allotted to the temple, is not *used*, is withdrawn from all merely utilitarian ends. Every seventh day is such a period of time. It is the "festival time", and it arises in this way and no other.

There can be no such thing in the world of "total labor" as space which is not used *on principle*; no such thing as a plot of ground, or a period of time withdrawn from use. There is in fact no *room* in the world of "total labor" either for divine worship, or for a feast: because the "worker's" world, the world of "labor" rests solely upon the principle of rational utilization. A "feast day" in that world is either a pause in the midst of work (and for the sake of work, of course), or in the case of "Labor Day", or whatever feast days of the world of "work" may be called, it is the very principle of work that is being celebrated—once again, work stops for

---

[1] *Reallexikon für Antike und Christentum*, 1942 Article "Arbeitsruhe".

the sake of work, and the feast is subordinated to "work". There can of course be games, *circenses*, circuses—but who would think of describing that kind of mass entertainment as festal?

It simply cannot be otherwise: the world of "work" and of the "worker" is a poor, impoverished world, be it ever so rich in material goods; for on an exclusively utilitarian basis, on the basis, that is, of the world of "work", genuine wealth, wealth which implies overflowing into superfluities, into unnecessaries, is just not possible. Wherever the superfluous makes its appearance it is immediately subjected to the rationalist, utilitarian principle of the world of work. And, as the traditional Russian saying puts it: work does not make one rich, but round-shouldered.

On the other hand, divine worship, of its very nature, creates a sphere of real wealth and superfluity, even in the midst of the direst material want—because sacrifice is the living heart of worship. And what does sacrifice mean? It means a voluntary offering freely given. It definitely does not involve utility; it is in fact absolutely antithetic to utility. Thus, the act of worship creates a store of real wealth that cannot be consumed by the workaday world. It sets up an area where calculation is thrown to the winds and goods are deliberately squandered, where usefulness is forgotten and generosity reigns. Such wastefulness is, we repeat, true wealth; the wealth of the festival time. And only in this festival time can leisure unfold and come to fruition.

Separated from the sphere of divine worship, of the cult of the divine, and from the power it radiates, leisure is as impossible as the celebration of a feast. Cut off from the worship of the divine, leisure becomes laziness and work inhuman.

That is the origin or source of all sham forms of leisure with their strong family resemblance to want of leisure and to sloth (in its old metaphysical and theological sense). The vacancy left by absence of worship is filled by mere killing of time and by boredom, which is directly related to inability to enjoy leisure; for one can only be bored if the spiritual power to be leisurely has been lost. There is an entry in Baudelaire's *Journal Intime* that is fearful in the precision of its cynicism: "One must work, if not from taste then at least from despair. For, to reduce everything to a single truth: work is less boring than pleasure."

And the counterpart to that is the fact that if real leisure is deprived of the support of genuine feast days and holy-days, work itself becomes inhuman: whether endured brutishly or "heroically" work is naked toil and effort without hope —it can only be compared to the labors of Sisyphus, that mythical symbol of the "worker" chained to his function, never pausing in his work, and never gathering any fruit from his labors.

In its extreme form the passion for work, naturally blind to every form of divine worship and often inimical to it, turns abruptly into its contrary, and work becomes a cult, becomes a religion. To work means to pray, Carlyle wrote, and he went on to say that fundamentally all genuine work is religion, and any religion that is not work ought to be left to Brahmins and dancing dervishes. Could anyone really pretend that that exotic nineteenth-century opinion was merely *bizarre* and not much more nearly a charter for the world of "total work"—that is on the way to becoming our world?

The celebration of divine worship, then, is the deepest of the springs by which leisure is fed and continues to be vital—though it must be remembered that leisure embraces everything which, without being *merely* useful, is an essential part of a full human existence.

In a period when divine worship is deeply felt and unites the whole social body and is, moreover, acknowledged as valid by all or nearly all, it might (perhaps) not be quite so necessary to discuss the foundation of leisure explicitly; and in so far as it was necessary to justify leisure in such periods it might (perhaps) be enough to dwell upon the purely humanistic arguments. But at a time when the nature of culture is no longer even understood, at a time when "the world of work" claims to include the whole field of human existence, and to be coterminous with it, it is necessary to go back to fundamentals in order to rediscover the ultimate justification of leisure.

An appeal to antiquity in the name of learning merely is virtually meaningless in times such as these; it is powerless against the enormous *pressure*, internal as well as external, of "the world of work". An appeal to Plato is no longer any good—unless one goes to the very roots of Plato (for we are concerned with roots, not with precedents, "influences"). Nor is it any use emphasizing that the traditions of philosophy go back to Plato's Academy, unless at the same time one accepts the religious character of the original "academy"; for Plato's Academy was a genuine religious association in which, for example, one of the members was explicitly appointed to prepare the sacrifice. Perhaps the reason why "purely academic" has sunk to mean something sterile, pointless and unreal is *because* the *schola* has lost its roots in religion and in divine worship. And so, instead of reality we get a world of make-believe, of intellectual *trompe l'œil*, and cultural tricks and traps and jokes, with here and there a "temple of the Muses" and a "holy of holies". Goethe certainly seems to have thought as much when he referred to the classicism of his day, in an astonishing phrase, declaring all the "*inventa* of antiquity" to be "matters *of faith*" which are now "fantastically copied out of pure fantasy".[2]

To repeat: today it is quite futile to defend the sphere of leisure in the last ditch but one. The sphere of leisure, it has already been said, is no less than the sphere of culture in so far as that word means everything that lies beyond the utilitarian world. Culture lives on religion through divine worship. And when culture itself is endangered, and leisure is called in question, there is only one thing to be done: to go back to the first and original source.

Such is, moreover, the meaning of the marvelous quotation from Plato placed at the beginning of this essay. The origin of the arts in worship, and of leisure derived from its celebration, is given in the form of a magnificent mythical image: man attains his true form and his upright attitude "in festive companionship with the gods".

But what—someone may well ask—are we *to do* about it?

Well, the considerations put forward in this essay were not designed to give advice and draw up a line of action; they were meant to make men think. Their aim has been to throw a little light on a problem which seems to me very important and very urgent, and is all too easily lost to sight among the immediate tasks in hand.

The object of this essay, then, is not to provide an immediate, practical guide to action. Nevertheless, there is one hope which ought, in conclusion, to be set down clearly —the fact is that in this sphere the decisive result is not to be achieved through action but can only be hoped for as dispensation. Our effort has been to regain some space for

---

[2] Wolfgang Goethe to Friedrich Wilhelm Riemer, March 26, 1814.

true leisure, to bring back a fundamentally right possession of leisure, "active leisure". The true difficulty in this often desperate effort is due to the fact that the ultimate root of leisure is not susceptible to the human will. Absolute affirmation of the universe cannot, strictly speaking, be based upon a voluntary resolve. Above all it cannot be "done" for the sake of a purpose lying outside itself. There are things that we cannot do "in order to . . ." or "so that. . . ." Either we do them not at all or we do them because they are right in saying that lack of leisure makes for illness. But just as certainly it is impossible to attempt to engage in leisure for health's sake. Such a reversal of the meaningful order of things is more than just unseemly; it simply cannot be done. Leisure cannot be achieved at all when it is sought as a means to an end, even though that end be "the salvation of Western civilization". Celebration of God in worship cannot be done unless it is done for its own sake. That most sublime form of affirmation of the world as a whole is the fountainhead of leisure.

Our hope is, in the first place, that the many signs *intra et extra muros* of a reawakening of the feeling for worship and its significance should not prove deceptive and misleading. For, to recapitulate: no one need expect a genuine religious worship, a *cultus*, to arise on purely human foundations, on foundations made by man; it is of the very nature of religious worship that its origin lies in a divine ordinance, a fact which is moreover implied in the quotation from Plato already referred to. No doubt the feeling for what has been ordained and laid down may increase, or it may lose its vitality. And that is the point toward which our hopes are directed —and not, of course, to the revival of some antiquated cult; and still less toward the foundation of a new religion! From those who see no hope along these lines (and hopelessness

along these lines, it must be conceded, could produce not a
few grounds in its defense)—from those who see nothing
worth hoping for here—we should certainly not expect to
find confidence in the future. This is a matter about which
it seems to me of the utmost importance to leave no doubt
in their minds.

Worship is either something "given", divine worship is
fore-ordained—or it does not exist at all. There can be no
question of founding a religion or instituting a religious *cultus*. And for the Christian there is, of course, no doubt in the
matter: *post Christum* there is only *one*, true and final form
of celebrating divine worship, the sacramental sacrifice of
the Christian Church. And moreover I think that anyone
inquiring into the facts of the case from a historical point
of view (whether he is a Christian or not) would be unable
to find any other worship whatsoever in the Europeanized
world.

The Christian *cultus*, unlike any other, is at once a sacrifice and a sacrament.[3] In so far as the Christian *cultus* is a
sacrifice held in the midst of the creation which is affirmed by
this sacrifice of the God-man—every day is a feast day; and
in fact the liturgy knows only feast days, even working days
being *feria*. In so far as the *cultus* is a *sacrament* it is celebrated
in visible signs. And the full power of worship will only be
felt if its sacramental character is realized in undiminished
form, that is, if the sign is fully visible. In leisure, as was
said, man oversteps the frontiers of the everyday workaday world, not in external effort and strain, but as though
lifted above it in ecstasy. That is the sense of the visibility
of the sacrament: that man is "carried away" by it, thrown
into "ecstasy". Let no one imagine for a moment that that

[3] *Summa Theologica*, III, 79, 5.

is a private and romantic interpretation. The Church has pointed to the meaning of the incarnation of the Logos in the self-same words: *ut dum visibiliter Deum cognoscimus, per hunc in invisibilium amorem rapiamur*, that we may be rapt into love of the invisible reality through the visibility of that first and ultimate sacrament: the Incarnation.

We therefore hope that this true sense of sacramental visibility may become so manifest in the celebration of the Christian *cultus* itself that in the performance of it man, "who is born to work", may truly be "transported" out of the weariness of daily labor into an unending holiday, carried away out of the straitness of the workaday world into the heart of the universe.

THE PHILOSOPHICAL ACT

*The reason, however, why the philosopher may be likened
to the poet is this: both are concerned with the marvelous.*

Thomas Aquinas

I

When a physicist sets out to define his science and asks what physics is, he is posing a preliminary question; in asking it he is plainly not at the experimental stage—not yet, or perhaps, no longer. But for anyone to ask, What does philosophizing mean? is quite certainly philosophy. The question is neither a preliminary one, nor is it just a postscript, one to be raised after the task has been accomplished—in some such form as: "What have we been doing?" The question occurs in the very midst of the undertaking. More precisely, I can say nothing whatsoever about philosophy without simultaneously saying something about man and his nature—and that, after all, is one of the central matters of philosophy. The opening question, What does philosophizing mean? is certainly philosophical.

But like all philosophical questions, it cannot be answered with complete finality. The answers to philosophical questions cannot, of their nature, be what Parmenides called "neatly rounded truths" and they cannot be picked and held in the hand like apples. The whole structure of philosophy and of philosophizing is different: it is a structure conditioned by hope; on which point there will be something to say later.

As a preliminary approach, however, it may be said that to philosophize is to act in such a way that one steps out of the workaday world. The next thing to do is to define what is meant by the workaday world, and then what is meant by going beyond that sphere.

The workaday world is the world of work, the utilitarian world, the world of the useful, subject to ends, open
to achievement and subdivided according to functions; it is
the world of demand and supply, of hunger and satiety. It
is dominated by a single end: the satisfaction of the "common need"; it is the world of work in so far as work is
synonymous with doing things for useful ends (so that effort and activity are characteristic of the workaday world).
Work is the process of satisfying the "common need"—an
expression that is by no means synonymous with the notion
of "common good". The "common need" is an essential
part of the "common good"; but the notion of "common
good" is far more comprehensive. For example, the "common good" requires (as Aquinas says[1]) that there should be
men who devote themselves to the "useless" life of contemplation, and, equally, that some men should philosophize.
—whereas it could not be said that contemplation or philosophy helps to satisfy the "common need".

More and more, at the present time, "common good"
and "common need" are identified; and (what comes to the
same thing) the world of work is becoming our entire world;
it threatens to engulf us completely, and the demands of the
world of work become greater and greater, till at last they
make a "total" claim upon the whole of human nature.

If, then, it is true to say that in the act of philosophizing
we transcend the world of work and are carried beyond the
world of work, it becomes plain that the question "What
does philosophizing mean?", which sounds so innocent at
first, so "theoretical", so abstract, is a very pressing and "actual" question at the present time. There is only one step in
thought (and geographically too) to finding ourselves in a

---

[1] Commentary on *Proverbs*, 4 d. 26, 1, 2.

world where work, labor, the process of satisfying the "common need", give their impress to the whole of human existence; inwardly as well as outwardly, the frontier between us and the world of "total work" is pressing in upon us—a world in which there is no room for philosophy or philosophizing in any true sense of the word: always assuming, of course, that to philosophize means to transcend the workaday world and that the philosophical act is incommensurable with the world of supply and demand, and the world of the "common need", and belongs elsewhere. And in fact, the more "total" the demands of the world of work, the more sharply and clearly do we see that philosophy is incommensurable with it. It may even be said that philosophy is conditioned at the present time by this situation and by the threat of the world of "total work", even more decisively than by its own proper problems. Philosophy—inevitably —becomes more and more distant, strange and remote; it even assumes the appearance of an intellectual luxury, and is felt to be a load on the social conscience, as the workaday world extends its claims and its sway over man.

The incommensurability of the philosophical act and the sphere of the workaday world needs, however, to be seen in its concrete aspects. It does not require any great effort of imagination to bring vividly to mind the things that dominate everyday life: we are plunged drastically in their midst. For so many people there is the daily struggle for a bare physical existence, for food, warmth, clothing and a roof over their head. In addition to our private worries and anxieties, and naturally influencing them, there is the need for reconstruction in Europe especially and more particularly in Germany—and the call for the organization of a new world. And alongside all this there is the struggle of nations for the goods of the earth. Everywhere there is a feeling of strain, of being overwrought and overdone—and this fatigue is only relieved in appearance by the breathless amusements or the brief pauses that punctuate its course: newspapers, a cinema, a cigarette. I do not have to detail what everyone knows. But there is no need either to concentrate on the present-day crisis and on the exaggerations which that involves. I mean quite simply the ordinary everyday world in which we live and play our part, with its very concrete ends to be achieved and realized, and which have to be squarely faced. Nothing, in fact, is further from my intention than in any way whatsoever to denigrate this world as though from some supposedly superior "philosophical" standpoint. Not a word need be wasted on that subject; that world is of course essentially part of man's world, being the very ground of his physical existence—without which, obviously, no one could philosophize!

But all the same, just try to imagine that all of a sudden, among the myriad voices in the factories and on the market square (Where can we get this, that or the other?)—that all of a sudden among those familiar voices and questions another voice were to be raised, asking: "Why, after all, should there be such a thing as being? Why not just nothing?"—the age-old, philosophical cry of wonder that Heidegger[2] calls the basic metaphysical question! Is it really necessary to emphasize how incommensurable philosophical inquiry and the world of work are? Anyone who asked that question without warning in the company of people whose minds hinge on necessities and material success would most likely be regarded as crazy. It is, however, in extreme cases such as this that the whole extent of the contrast comes to

[2] Martin Heidegger, *Was ist Metaphysik?* p. 22. (Frankfort, 1943.)

light: and then it is clear that the question transcends the workaday world and leads beyond it.

A properly philosophical question always pierces the dome that encloses the bourgeois workaday world, though it is not the only way of taking a step beyond that world. Poetry no less than philosophy is incommensurable with it.

> How sweet I roam'd from field to field
> And tasted all the summer's pride,
> Till I the Prince of love beheld
> Who in the sunny beams did glide![3]

Surely the sudden effect of poetry in the realm of means and ends comes as strange and remote as a philosophical question. Nor is it otherwise with prayer. Perhaps it is still understandable that men should say: "Give us this day our daily bread", but what of the words of the *Gloria: Gratias agimus tibi propter magnam gloriam tuam?*—can words such as these be understood in the context of the "rational-useful" and of a utilitarian organization? Man also steps beyond the chain of ends and means, that binds the world of work, in love, or when he takes a step toward the frontier of existence, deeply moved by some existential experience, for this, too, sends a shock through the world of relationships, whatever the occasion may be—perhaps the close proximity of death. The act of philosophizing, genuine poetry, any aesthetic encounter, in fact, as well as prayer, springs from some shock. And when such a shock is experienced, man senses the non-finality of this world of daily care; he transcends it, takes a step beyond it.

The philosophical act, the religious act, the aesthetic act, as well as the existential shocks of love and death, or any

[3] William Blake.

other way in which man's relation to the world is convulsed and shaken—all these fundamental ways of acting belong naturally together, by reason of the power which they have in common of enabling a man to break through and transcend the workaday world.

Plato, as everyone knows, virtually identified philosophy and Eros. And in regard to the similarity of philosophy and poetry, there is the little-known and curious saying of Aquinas which occurs in his commentary on the *Metaphysics* of Aristotle: The philosopher, he there says, is related to the poet in that both are concerned with *mirandum*, with wonder, with marveling and with that which makes us marvel.[4] That saying is not altogether easily plumbed, and it acquires added significance because, as thinkers, Aristotle and Aquinas are both cool-headed, sensible men, altogether averse from any kind of romantic blurring of the orders. Thus poetry and philosophy are more closely related to one another than any of the sciences to philosophy; both, equally, are aimed, as one might say, at wonder (and wonder does not occur in the workaday world)—and this by virtue of the power of transcending the everyday world, a power common to poetry and philosophy. But to that we shall return again.

The family resemblance between all these acts is so significant and of such importance that whenever *one* member is denied in principle, the remainder cannot live—and in a totalitarian world of work every form and manner of transcendence is bound to wither (would perish, indeed, if human nature could be destroyed or altered entirely): for where the religions spirit is not tolerated, where there is no room for poetry and art, where love and death are robbed

---

[4] Commentary on the *Metaphysics*. 1, 3.

of all significant effect and reduced to the level of a banality, philosophy will never prosper.

But worse, even, than the silencing or simple extinction of these experiences of transcendence is their transformation, their degradation, into sham and spurious forms; and pseudo-realizations of these fundamental acts most certainly exist, giving the appearance of piercing the dome of everyday life. It is possible to pray in such a way that one does not transcend the world, in such a way that the divine is degraded to a functional part of the workaday world. Religion can be debased into magic. Then it is no longer devotion to the divine, but an attempt to master it. Prayer can be perverted in this way, into a sort of technique whereby life under the dome is feasible. Moreover, love too can assume a debased form in which all the powers of devotion are bent to serve the ends of a limited ego. That debasement springs from timid self-defense against the shock of the greater, deeper world that can be entered only by one who truly loves. Then again there is a pseudo-art and a spurious poetry which, instead of bursting through the vault of the workaday world, merely paint deceptive ornamentation upon the inner surface of the dome. Much utilitarian verse, whether private or political in nature, more or less undisguisedly serves the ends of the workaday world. That sort of poetry does not go beyond anything, does not even pretend to try. (It is clear that genuine philosophy has more in common with the exact sciences than with any such pseudo-poetry.) And finally, there is even a pseudo-philosophy, and its mark is the same: it does not transcend the workaday world. At one point, it will be remembered, Socrates asks Protagoras the Sophist,[5]

[5] *Protagoras*, 318f.

"What do you really teach the young who crowd to your lectures?", and Protagoras replies: "To be well informed—both in their own affairs, namely how best to manage one's house and run one's estate, and in matters concerning the State; how best to be effective in speaking and in acting." That is the classical program of philosophy considered as a profession, as training: a pseudo-philosophy that will never pierce the dome.

And the worst of it all is, that these spurious forms combine—not indeed to go beyond the workaday world, but on the contrary—to screw down the dome more firmly than ever, to close every window—and then man really is imprisoned in the world of work. These deceptive forms, and especially a spurious philosophy, are far worse, far more hopeless, than the worldly person's naïve refusal to recognize anything outside the commonplace. Nevertheless, a man who is thus caught up and entangled in the web of everyday life may still be shaken, one day, by some profound emotion, whether it comes to him in the form of a philosophical question, or a poem, or a face. But a sophist, a pseudo-philosopher, can never be shaken.

But let us return to the question we began with. If we inquire into the real nature of philosophy, we are asking a question that goes beyond the workaday world. Clearly, our present times add a particularly keen historical edge to the question, to the doubt, if you like; for never before in the history of the West has the world of work advanced such bold claims, insisted so strongly on its own "totality". But the problem is not limited to our times. We are dealing with a basic and ever-recurring misunderstanding.

When the Thracian Maid saw Thales of Miletus, the stargazer, fall into the cistern she laughed; and Plato accepted her laughter as the answer of hard-headed common sense to philosophy. The history of European philosophy might be said to begin with that legend. Ever and again, so we are told in the *Theaetetus*, "ever and again" the philosopher is the occasion of laughter: "not only the Maids of Thrace, but the many laugh at him because, a stranger to the world, he falls into a cistern and into many another embarrassment."[6]

Now Plato does not express himself only, or even principally, in explicit words or formal arguments; rather, he speaks by means of the characters he creates. There is, for instance, Apollodorus, a subsidiary character in the *Phaidon* and the *Symposium*, as one might easily be led to suppose. Apollodorus is one of those uncritical, enthusiastic youngsters who follow in the wake of Socrates and who are, perhaps, intended to suggest Plato himself as a young man. We are told in the *Phaidon* that when Socrates drank the hemlock, Apollodorus was the only one present to burst into tears: "of course you know him and his way of carrying on."[7] In the *Symposium*,[8] Apollodorus himself recounts how, for years, he had been eager to know what Socrates had said and done each day; "formerly I went about, driven along by events, and thought I was being very busy, while all the time I was more wretched than anyone." Then he met Socrates, and devoted himself wholeheartedly to him and to philosophy. The whole town began to talk of him as "crazed"; he got furious with everyone, and even with himself, with the exception always of Socrates. He went about everywhere, naïvely announcing that he was "happy beyond all measure" as long as he could talk about philosophy or hear others talk about it; and then grew miserable at failing to achieve his ambition and be like Socrates.

[6] *Theaetetus*, 174.
[7] *Phaidon*, 59.
[8] *Symposium*, 172f.

Then, one day, Apollodorus meets some old friends, the
very ones in fact, who call him mad. And, as Plato is careful
to note, they are businessmen, only interested in money,
who know how to make and produce things, and who are
convinced that they are "getting things done". These friends
of his, nevertheless, ask Apollodorus to tell them something
about the banquet that was held in the poet Agathon's house,
and the speeches on love that followed. It is clear enough
that these businessmen, with their belief in success, felt not
the least need to be instructed in the meaning of the world
and existence—least of all by Apollodorus. All they cared
about, probably, was the wit and elegance of the speeches, a
well-turned phrase or a delicate innuendo. Nor, for the matter of that, has Apollodorus any illusion about their "philosophical leanings". Quite the reverse. He says straight out
that he is sorry for them—"because you think you are doing something when you are really doing nothing. Now,
you may, perhaps, think that I am badly off, and I dare say
you are right on that score; but I not only believe you are
badly off: I know it for certain." But all the same, he is not
afraid of telling them what was said: he simply cannot keep
quiet: "if you really want to know, then I must tell you"—
even though it confirms them in thinking him crazy. And
then Apollodorus tells them—the *Symposium*! The *Symposium* is a story told by Apollodorus in indirect speech. I cannot help feeling that too little attention is paid to the fact
that Plato puts his profoundest thoughts into the mouth
of an enthusiast, an overzealous, uncritical, somewhat fan-
tastic youngster, hardly more than an undergraduate—and
what is more before an audience of hardheaded businessmen
who were neither capable nor, indeed, desirous, of taking
what was said seriously. There is an element of hopelessness,

of despair almost, about the situation—and Plato's meaning
seems to be that, faced with that situation, only the unflinch-
ing eagerness of youth in its search for wisdom could hope
to prevail: a situation in which only a genuine *philosophia*
could survive. But however that may be, Plato could not
have emphasized the incommensurability of philosophizing
and the self-sufficient world of work more plainly.

But that is only the negative aspect of the incommensurability in question; the other aspect is: freedom. Philosophy
is "useless" and unusable in matters of everyday life where
things are to be turned to account and results achieved: that
is one point. It is quite another thing, however, to say that
it serves no purpose whatsoever beyond itself and its own
end or that it can never be used apart from its own end.
Philosophy is not functional knowledge but, as Newman
said, "the knowledge of a gentleman";[9] not a useful knowledge, but a "free" knowledge. Freedom, here, means that
philosophical knowledge is not legitimized by its usefulness
or usableness, or by virtue of its social function, or with reference to the "common need". This is the selfsame sense in
which "freedom" was used in the phrase "artes liberales",
the liberal arts—in contradistinction to the "artes serviles",
the servile arts which, as Aquinas says, are "ordered to the
satisfaction of a need through activity."[10] Philosophy has always been regarded as the freest of all the liberal arts (and in
the Middle Ages the philosophical faculty was even named
after the artes liberales: ordo artistarum, the faculty of liberal
arts).

And so it comes to the same thing if I say that the act of

[9] John Henry Cardinal Newman, *Idea of a University*, V, 6.
[10] Aquinas, ibid., 1, 3.

philosophizing transcends the world of work, or if I say that philosophical knowledge is unusable, or if I call philosophy a "liberal art".

The special sciences, it should be noted, are only free in this sense in so far as they are pursued philosophically. That is actually, as well as historically, the meaning of academic freedom (for academic, in this case, means philosophical or it means nothing); and any claim to academic freedom, in the strict sense of the word, can only arise in so far as "academic" fulfills its philosophical character. And actually, as well as historically, academic freedom goes by the board in exactly the same degree in which the philosophical character of academic studies is lost; in other words, to the extent to which the total claim of the world of work invades the academic sphere. That is the metaphysical root of the matter; and the so-called "political" invasion is only a consequence and a symptom.

It should, however, most certainly be added that this failure is the direct fruit of philosophy itself, of modern philosophy. And with one more word on that subject, we will conclude this chapter.

But first, one word on the freedom of philosophy, as distinguished from the sciences: "freedom" being understood to mean "not being at the disposal of external aims and ends". The different branches of science are "free" in this sense, provided only that they are pursued philosophically and in so far as they share the freedom of philosophy. "Knowledge is free", writes Newman, "in the truest sense, as soon as and in so far as it is philosophical."[11] In themselves, however, the various branches of science may perfectly well be placed "at the disposal of external aims and

---

[11] Newman, *Idea of a University*, V, 6.

ends", and they can always be "applied" in order to satisfy a need (which is Aquinas' definition of a servile art).

To take a concrete example. The government of a country may quite well say: "In order to carry out our five-year plan, we need physicists trained in these particular branches of their science, men who will help to put us ahead of other countries"; or: "We need medical research students to discover a more efficient cure for the flu." Something of this kind may be said or done without violating the essential nature of the sciences in question. But: "At the moment we need philosophers to . . ."—well, what? There is of course only one conclusion—"to elaborate, defend and demonstrate the following ideology"—it is only possible to talk or write in such terms if philosophy is being strangled to death at the very same moment. Exactly the same thing would be true if someone in authority were to say: "At the moment, we need some poets to . . ."—well, and "to what?" And again, there is only one possible answer: to prove (as the saying goes) the pen mightier than the sword in the service of some idea dictated by the state. And that, obviously, is the death of poetry. The moment such a thing happened, poetry would cease to be poetry, and philosophy would cease to be philosophy.

But this is not to say that there is no sort of connection between the fulfillment of the "common good" and the philosophy taught in a country! Only the relationship can never be established or regulated from the point of view of the general good: when a thing contains its own end, or is an end in itself, it can never be made to serve as a means to any other end—just as no one can love someone "in order that".

The fact that philosophy cannot be put at the disposal of some end other than its own is intimately connected with its

theoretical character and is, indeed, identical with it—and
that is a point which is of the greatest importance, which
ought to be stressed. To philosophize is the purest form of
speculari, of *theorein*, it means to look at reality purely receptively—in such a way that things are the measure and the
soul is exclusively receptive. Whenever we look at being
philosophically, we discourse purely "theoretically" about
it, in a manner, that is to say, untouched in any way whatsoever by practical considerations, by the desire to change
it; and it is in this sense that philosophy is said to be above
any and every "purpose".

The realization of *theoria* in this sense is, however, linked
to another presupposition. It requires a specific relation to
the world, a relation prior to any conscious construction and
foundation. We can only be theoretical in the full sense of the
word (where it means a receptive vision untouched by the
smallest intention to alter things, and even a complete readiness to make the will's consent or dissent dependent upon
the reality we perceive through the recognition of which we
give our yea or our nay)—we can only be "theoretical" in
this undiluted sense, so long as the world is something other
(and something more) than a field for human activity, its
material, or even its raw material. We can only be "theoretical" in the full sense of the word if we are able to look upon
the world as the creation of an absolute spirit, as something
that deserves our reverence. "Pure theory", which is part of
the essence of philosophy, can thrive only in such soil. And
thus the freedom to philosophize and the act of philosophizing itself are made psychologically possible by an ultimate
tie of the most profound kind. It should scarcely surprise
us that the weakening of that tie (by virtue of which the
world is viewed as a Creation and not as material for man

to act upon) should keep pace with the breakdown of the
theoretical character of philosophy, with its loss of prestige
vis-à-vis mere functioning, and with the decay of philosophy
itself. There is a direct road from "Knowledge is power"
—and Bacon's other statement that the purpose of knowledge is to furnish man with new inventions and gadgets[12]
—to Descartes' more explicitly polemical statement in the
Discourse that he intended to replace the old "theoretical"
philosophy by a practical kind, so that we men might make
ourselves the "masters and owners of nature".[13] That road
leads on to Marx's well-known declaration: hitherto philosophy has been concerned with interpreting the world, but
what matters is to change it.

This assault upon philosophy's theoretical character is the
historical road of philosophy's suicide. And that assault arises
from the world's being seen more and more as mere raw
material for human activity. Once the world is no longer
regarded as Creation, there cannot be "theoria" in the full
meaning of the word. The loss of "theoria" means *eo ipso*
the loss of the freedom of philosophy: philosophy then becomes a function within society, solely practical, and it must
of course justify its existence and role among the functions
of society; and finally, in spite of its name, it appears as a
form of work or even of "labor". Whereas my thesis (which
should by now be emerging plainly with its contours well
defined), is that the essence of "philosophizing" is that it
transcends the world of work. It is a thesis which comprehends the assertion of the theoretical character of philosophy
and its freedom; it does not, of course, in any way deny or

[12] Francis Bacon, *Novum Organum*, I, 3; I, 81.
[13] René Descartes, *Discours de la Méthode*, 6.

ignore the world of work (indeed it assumes its prior and necessary existence), but it does affirm that a real philosophy is grounded in belief, that man's real wealth consists, not in satisfying his needs, not in becoming "the master and owner of nature", but in seeing what is and the whole of what is, in seeing things not as useful or useless, serviceable or not, but simply as being. The basis of this conception of philosophy is the conviction that the greatness of man consists in his being *capax universi*.[14]

The ultimate perfection attainable to us, in the minds of the philosophers of Greece, was this: that the order of the whole of existing things should be inscribed in our souls. And this conception was afterward absorbed into the Christian tradition in the conception of the beatific vision: "What do they not see, who see him who sees all things?"[15]

---

[14] Aquinas, *Quaest. disp. de veritate*, 2, 2.
[15] Gregory the Great, quoted by Aquinas, ibid.

II

To philosophize, then, is to take a step beyond the everyday world of work.

Now the meaning of a step is best defined in relation to its goal, to the "whither" rather than to the "whence". Where does philosophizing carry us? Obviously, in going beyond the world of work, it crosses a frontier: what sort of a world lies beyond? And how are the two worlds related, the world into which the act of philosophizing carries us, and the world which this same act transcends? Could it be said that the former is the "essential" world, and the world of work the inessential; is it the "whole" as opposed to the part; or is it reality as contrasted with appearance?

However these questions may be answered in detail, one thing is clear: both worlds, the world of work and the realm into which the act of philosophizing carries us—*both* belong to the world of man which is clearly, therefore, a many-storied structure.

Our next question, then, is: What kind of a world is man's world?—a question which patently cannot be answered without reference to the nature of man. And in order to achieve some degree of clarity, we must begin from the beginning and start from the bottom.

Every living thing lives in a world, in "its" world, and "has" a world in which it lives. To live means to be "in" the world. Though a stone, you may say, is surely "in" the world? Everything there "is", is "in" the world, surely? But let us stick to the stone, for the moment, lifeless, lying about

with other things, next to other things and surely "in" the
world. "In", "next to", "with", all prepositions, words indicating a relation: though the stone is not really related to
the world "in" which it is, nor to the things "next to" which
it lies, nor to those "with" which it is in the world. A relationship in the proper sense of the word, is a link established
from inside to something external; relations can only exist
where there is an "inside", where there is that dynamic center from which all activity springs and to which all that is received and all that is undergone can be collectively referred.
In this qualitative sense (one cannot, of course, speak of the
"inside" of a stone—one can only speak of the "inside" of
a stone with reference to the disposal of its parts), the "inside" is the power by virtue of which a relation to something
external is possible; inwardness is the capacity to establish
relations and to communicate. And what of "world"? Well,
world means the same thing as a range of relations. Only
a being capable of having relations, only a being of whom
"inner" as well as "outer" may be predicated—and this in
its turn means a living being—has a world. Only a living
being exists within a range of relationships.

There is a fundamental difference between relations thus
conceived and the relation which results from the proximity of stones in a heap by the roadside, though technically
one can, of course, speak of stones neighboring one upon
the other. That form of relation is, again, different from the
relation between a plant and the nutriment it draws through
its roots out of the ground, for then the relation is not solely
spatial, an objective fact and nothing more, it is a real relation in the primary sense of the word, in the active reflexive
sense of "relating itself": the nourishment in the ground
and in the air is absorbed and assimilated into the sphere
of the plant's life by the dynamic center of the plant, and

its power of establishing relations. All that constitutes the plant's range of relations makes its world. A plant, in fact, has a world, and a stone has not.

That, then, is the first point: the world is a field of relations. To have a world is to be the center, the coordinator, of a field of relations. The second point is: the higher the *order* of a being, the more embracing and wider its power of establishing relations—the greater the field of relations within its power. This may also be expressed by saying that the higher a being stands in the order of reality, in the hierarchic order of being, the wider and deeper its world.

The lowest world, the first step in the hierarchy, is that of the plant which does not extend its spatial world beyond the sphere of touch. The animal's world is higher than this and corresponds to the animal's greater power of establishing relations. The animal's capacity to establish relations is greater in so far as it is capable of being sensibly and sensually aware; "to be aware" of a thing is an entirely new mode of relating itself to a thing, unknown in the plant world, a new manner of relating itself to the "outside".

It is by no means true, however, that everything an animal is able, abstractly speaking, to see or to hear, belongs to its "world"; animals possessed of eyes do not actually see, nor could they see, everything that is visible in their "surroundings". And "surroundings", even "surroundings" which could "in themselves" be apprehended, do not yet constitute a "world". Though this view was far from generally held until Jacob von Uexküll, the biologist, published his findings. Up to that time, as Uexküll himself puts it,[1] "it was generally assumed that all animals with eyes saw the same objects." But Uexküll found that this was far from

[1] *Der unsterbliche Geist in der Natur*, p. 63 (1938).

being the case. "The animal's 'environment' is something altogether different from the natural scene; it more nearly resembles a small, poorly furnished room."[2] And he gives the following example: one might have supposed that a crow, "with eyes in its head", could see a grasshopper (after all, a very desirable object to a crow) at least when there was one before its eyes. But not at all! And here I will quote Uexküll:

> A crow is utterly unable to see a grasshopper that is not moving . . . We are perhaps inclined to suppose that although the shape of a grasshopper is familiar to the crow, it is unable to recognize a grasshopper if a blade of grass cuts across it, it cannot recognize it as the "unity" grasshopper—just as we find it quite difficult to recognize a familiar object in a picture-puzzle. On this assumption it is only when the grasshopper jumps that its shape becomes recognizable and dissociates itself from the surrounding images. But further experiments lead one to suppose that a crow simply does not know the shape of a motionless grasshopper and is so constituted that it can only apprehend the moving form. That would explain why so many insects feign death. If their motionless form simply does not exist in the field of vision of their enemies, then by shamming death they drop out of that world with absolute certainty and cannot be found even though searched for.[3]

Animals are perfectly adapted to their sharply defined and delimited environment—perfectly adapted to it, but equally, imprisoned within it, so that they cannot overstep the frontier in any way whatsoever: they cannot even find an object though armed with senses that are apparently well adapted

[2] Ibid., p. 76.

[3] Uexküll-Kriszat, *Streifzüge durch die Umwelten von Tieren und Menschen*, p. 40.

to the purpose, unless, that is, the object fits completely into their selected, partial world. This selected reality, selected by the biological necessities either of the individual or the genus or species, so limited and sharply defined, is what Uexküll calls *Umwelt*: "environment" in contrast to "surroundings" and in contrast to "world", as appeared from the subsequent discussion of the question. An animal's field of relationships is not its "surroundings" and certainly not "the world". Its field of relationships is a very clearly delimited "environment": a world from which something has been omitted, in which its inmate is enclosed and to which it is, at the same time, perfectly adapted.

All this may seem, at first sight, somewhat distant from the theme with which we began: "What do we mean by philosophizing?" But it is not simply a digression. We had reached the point of asking about man's world, and that is where Uexküll's conception of "environment" is relevant— for (according to Uexküll) our human world "cannot claim to be any more real than the animal's world";[4] man, then, is limited by his environment in exactly the same way as an animal, that is to say, he is limited to a selected environment assembled, as it were, by natural selection and biological necessity; he is incapable of apprehending anything and, even though searching for it, of finding anything outside his environment—like the crow that cannot find a motionless grasshopper. (The question does arise, however, as to how a creature limited to its own environment and imprisoned so effectively within it could study the theory of environment.)

But we do not wish to engage in a disputation here; let us leave this matter for the time being and fix our attention

---

[4] *Die Lebenslehre*, p. 131.

upon man and the world that is related to him: What are the
nature and the powers of man's capacity for relationships?
We have already said that, by comparison with plants, the
perceptive faculty of animals brought new and more exten-
sive powers of relating into the world. May we not say that
the form of knowing peculiar to man, which has always
been called man's power of cognition, has also introduced
a new mode of relating, one from which both animal and
plant organisms are barred? To this essentially new capacity for relations there must, surely, correspond a field or
world, of other dimensions no doubt, answering to that capacity. The answer to this question is that in the tradition
of Western philosophy, the capacity for spiritual knowledge
has always been understood to mean the power of establishing relations with the whole of reality, with all things
existing; that is how it has been defined, and it is conceived
as a definition more than as a description. *Spirit*, it might
be said, is not only defined as incorporeal, but as the power
and capacity to relate itself to the totality of being. *Spirit*, in
fact, is a capacity for relations of such all-embracing power
that its field of relations transcends the frontiers of all and
any "environment". To talk of "environment" where spirit
is concerned, is a misunderstanding, for its field of relations is "the world", and by its very nature it breaks the
bounds of any "environment"; it abolishes both adaptation
and imprisonment. Therein lies, at one and the same time,
the liberating force and the danger inherent in the nature of
spirit.

In summing up what he has said about the soul in the *De
anima*, Aristotle says:[5] "The soul is, fundamentally, everything that is"—words which were to become a favorite tag

---

[5] *De anima*, 3, 8 (431b).

in the Middle Ages: *anima est quodammodo omnia*, the soul is in a certain sense all things, the all. "In a certain sense" means to say in so far as it knowingly places itself in relation to the whole of being (and to know something means to become identical with the known reality, though this is not the place to say more on that score). The spiritual soul, Aquinas says, in his considerations on truth, is meant to fit in with all being, *convenire cum omni ente.*[6] "Every other being takes only a limited part in being", whereas the spiritual being is "capable of grasping the whole of being".[7] And "because there is spirit, it is possible for the perfection of the whole of being to exist in one being."[8]

That is the tradition of Western philosophy: to have spirit, or to be spirit, means to exist in the midst of the whole of reality and before the whole of being, the whole of being *vis-à-vis de l'univers.* Spirit does not exist in "a" world, nor in "its" world, but in "the" world, "the" world in the sense of *visibilia omnia et invisibilia.*

"The whole of reality" and "spirit" are reciprocal, corresponding concepts. One cannot have the one without the other. The attempt has been made to attribute to man superiority to environment *without* speaking of his spirituality. One writer has gone even further, asseverating that the fact of man's having a world and not just an environment has no connection with the other fact, that man is a being endowed with spirit. The writer in question is Arnold Gehlen, who presents this thesis in his much-discussed book, *Der Mensch; Seine Natur und seine Stellung in der Welt.*[9] Gehlen quite rightly opposes Uexküll: man, he declares, is not

[6] *Quaest. disp. de veritate*, 1, 1.
[7] *Summa contra Gentes*, 3, 112.
[8] *Quaest. disp. de veritate*, 2, 2.
[9] Berlin, 1940.

locked in an environment as are animals; man is free of environment and receptive to the whole universe. But, Gehlen continues, this distinction between the animal as a creature of environment and man as a being receptive to the world does not rest "upon the characteristic . . . of spirit. . . ." Here he is wrong: the very power to "have" a world *is* the spirit. Spirit is by nature the capacity to apprehend a world!

To the philosophers of the past—to Plato, Aristotle, Augustine, and Thomas Aquinas—the concepts of "spirit" and "world" (in the sense of the whole of reality) are not only interrelated; their correspondence is complete. These philosophers not only held that "spirit is relatedness to the totality of existing things", but also that all existing things are essentially related to spirit. Moreover, they formulated that relation in such precise terms that at first we scarcely dare to take them at their word. Not only, they said, is it of the nature of the spirit for its frame of reference to be the totality of existing things; but it is also of the nature of existing things for them to lie within spirit's frame of reference. Furthermore, in the philosophical tradition of which I am speaking, it comes to the same thing whether I say, "Things have being" or whether I say, "Things exist in the spirit's frame of reference." In saying this, of course, I do not refer to some vague, abstract "spirituality", but to a personal spirit, to an immanent power of establishing relationships. Nor do I refer to God alone, but equally to the limited, created human spirit.

That is what is meant by the proposition *omne ens est verum* (everything that is, is true)—though we have almost ceased to understand it—and by the complementary proposition that being and truth are interchangeable concepts. (What does truth mean, where things are concerned, the truth of things? "A thing is true" means: it is known and knowable, known to the absolute spirit, knowable to the spirit that is not absolute. Unfortunately I can only ask you to accept that statement as it stands; this is not the place to embark on its interpretation.[10] For our present purpose the important thing about the concept "the truth of things" is that it means that the essence of things is to be related to spirit.)

To sum up: the world of a spiritual being is the totality of existing things; and their correspondence is so complete that it is both essential to spirit (spirit is the power of embracing the totality of being) and equally it is essential to things themselves ("to be" means "to be in relation to spirit").

We found, in the course of our considerations, a hierarchic ladder of "worlds" of which the world of plants was the lowest, limited to the spatial, to the things it touched; next comes the environment of animals; and finally the world corresponding or coordinated to spirit, that includes and transcends all these other partial, limited worlds: *the* world as the totality of being. And this hierarchy of worlds, of fields of relations, corresponds, as we saw, to the hierarchy of the graduated powers and capacities to establish relations; so that the greater the capacity for relations the greater the dimensions of the coordinated field, until that field becomes (for spirit) "the" world.

To this double chain of steps or grades we must now add a third, structural, element: the greater the power of establishing relations the greater the degree of inwardness; the lowest degree of relations corresponds not only to the most limited world but also to the most restricted form of inwardness —while spirit, which corresponds to the totality of being,

---

[10] See Josef Pieper, *Wahrheit der Dinge* (1948). English ed.: *Living the Truth* (San Francisco: Ignatius Press, 1989). This volume contains *Reality and the Good* and *The Truth of All Things*—TRANS.

is also the highest form of inwardness, what Goethe called *"wohnen in sich selbst"*—dwelling in oneself. The more embracing the power with which to relate oneself to objective being, the more deeply that power needs to be anchored in the inner self of the subject so as to counterbalance the step it takes outside. And where this step attains a world that is in principle complete (with totality as its aim) the reflective self, characteristic of spirit, is also reached. The two together constitute spirit: not only the capacity to relate oneself to the whole of reality, to the whole world, but an unlimited capacity of living in oneself, the gift of self-reliance and independence that, in the philosophical tradition of Europe, have always been regarded as the attributes of the human person, of being a person. To have a world, to be related to the totality of existing things, can only be the attribute of a being whose substance is within himself—not a "what" but a "who", a self, a person.

It is now time we looked back again to the questions we began with. There were two questions, an immediate and a wider: the immediate question concerned the nature of man's world and the wider question was "what do we mean by philosophizing?"

Before taking them up again formally, there is just one more observation to be made on the structure of the world in the context of "spirit": it is not, of course, merely in the matter of quantitative size that the world in this context is differentiated from the "environment" of plants and animals —a fact which many discussions about world and environment so often overlook. The world coordinated to spirit is not merely the world of all things but at the same time of the essence of things. And that is why an animal's environment is limited: because the essence of things is concealed from it. And, contrariwise, it is only because man, being a spirit, is capable of attaining the essence of things, that he can embrace the totality of things—this interrelationship was traditionally expressed in the following terms: both the essence of things and the universe is "universal"; and in the words of Aquinas, "the spiritual soul is capable of the infinite because it can grasp the universal."[11] To know the universal essence of things is to reach a point of view from which the whole of being and all existing things become visible; at the same time the spiritual outpost thus reached by knowing the essence of things enables man to look upon the landscape of the whole universe.

But to return to the question, first of all the preliminary question about man's world. Is the world thus coordinated to spirit, man's world? The answer to this is that man's world is the whole of reality; man lives in and is confronted by the whole of reality, *vis-à-vis de l'univers*—in so far as he is spirit. But not only is he not pure spirit, he is finite spirit; and consequently the essence of things and their totality is not given to him fully and completely in the purity of the concept: but "in hope", and on that point I shall have something to add in the next chapter.

In the meanwhile let us consider the implications of saying that man is not pure spirit. It is a statement that can be made in different keys, with many variations of tone, so that the emphasis falls at a different point and strikes from a different angle—a note of regret, for instance, is by no manner of speaking unusual, and indeed Christians as well as non-Christians consider it "quite especially Christian". It can also be expressed so as to imply that while man is not pure spirit, the "real man" is, "of course", the spiritual soul. Neither tendency, however, has any ground in the Western

[11] *Summa Theologica*, I, 76, 5 ad 4.

tradition of Christendom. There is a passage in St. Thomas
that points the argument with all desirable clarity. He puts to
himself the following objection: The end of man is, surely,
perfect similarity with God, and the soul separated from the
body will be more like God than the soul joined to the body,
since God is incorporeal. The soul in its final state of happiness, therefore, will be separated from the body. That is
the objection Aquinas uses in order to introduce the thesis
"the real man is the spiritual soul", attired, as it were, in
all the finery of a theological argument. To that objection
he replies as follows: "The soul united to the body is more
like God than the soul separated from the body because it
possesses its own nature more perfectly"[12]—an answer that
is by no means easily digested, for it implies not only that
man is corporeal, but that in a certain sense, even the soul
is corporeal.

But if that be so, if man is *essentially* not pure spirit, not
spirit only, and if man is a being in whom plant, animal and
spiritual life are fused together and thus fused not merely
as the consequence of some failure on his part to attain his
end, of some lagging behind his destiny—if that be so, then
he cannot be expected to live exclusively or essentially face
to face with the whole world of reality; on the contrary, he
must live in a field of relationships where world and environment are necessarily incorporated, one within the other,
and corresponding to the complex nature of man (as opposed to the simple nature of animal or pure spirit).

That is why man cannot live permanently "beneath the
stars", *vis-à-vis de l'univers*; he needs the roof of the familiar
over his head, the surroundings of everyday life, the sensual proximity of the concrete, the regularity of habit and

---

[12] *Quaest. disp. de potentia Dei*, 5, 10 ad 5.

custom. In a word: a full human life calls for environment, too, in the differentiated sense we have given it, in which environment is not "the world".

At the same time it is one of the characteristics of man, a corporeal and spiritual being, that it should be his spiritual soul which informs the physical and sensitive realms—to such a degree that taking food in man and animal are two utterly different things (quite apart from the fact that in the human sphere a "meal" may have a spiritual or even a religious character). It is so true that the spiritual soul informs the whole of man's nature that even when a man "vegetates" it is ultimately only possible because he is spiritual—a cabbage can't vegetate. Equally, when man shuts himself up in his environment, in the sphere defined and limited by his immediate needs, the degeneration that follows is only possible because spiritual degeneration is possible. The really human thing is to see the stars above the roof, to preserve our apprehension of the universality of things in the midst of the habits of daily life, and to see "the world" above and beyond our immediate environment.

And with that we are back unawares at our first question: "What do we mean by philosophizing?" It means to experience the fact that our immediate surroundings, prescribed as they are by the aims and needs of life, not only can be, but must be broken in upon (not only once but ever and again), by the disturbing call of "the world", of the whole world and the everlasting and essential images of things mirrored by reality. To philosophize—and what we asked was whither the philosophical act carries us when it transcends the workaday world—to philosophize means to step beyond the sectional, partial environment of the workaday world into a position *vis-à-vis de l'univers*: a step that takes one into the open, for the heavens are not a roof over a man's head—though one ought always to leave the door open behind one, for a man cannot live like that continuously. Who, in fact, would want to emigrate for good and all out of the Thracian maid's world or think it possible to do so: for it would mean leaving the human world altogether. And in fact one could apply to philosophizing the words that Aquinas used of contemplation when he spoke of it as something really superhuman: *non proprie humana, sed superhumana*.[13] To be sure, man himself is in a measure superhuman and is, as Pascal says, infinitely above man (every attempt to provide a smooth definition of man is bound to fail).

But this is not the place to pursue a thought that threatens to topple us over into enthusiasm. Our question is "what do we mean by philosophizing", and it is that question we want to answer, quite concretely and simply, and helped thereto by all that we have already said. What distinguishes a philosophical question from one which is not philosophical? To philosophize, we said, meant fixing our mind's eye on the totality of being, "the world". Now, is *the* philosophical question (and it alone) the question which explicitly and formally concerns the totality of being and of things? Of course not. But it is certainly true that the distinctive mark of a philosophical question is that it cannot be put, or weighed, or answered (in so far as an answer is possible at all) without bringing into play "God and the world", without implied reference to all that is.

Let us take a concrete example. The question "what are we doing, here and now?" can obviously be taken in a number of different ways; it *can* be given a philosophical meaning. It can have a purely superficial relevancy, concerned solely with a technical answer that deals with organization. "What

[13] *Quaest. disp. de virtutibus cardinalibus*, 5, 1.

is taking place here?"—"A philosophical lecture in the Summer School held at Bonn." That is a clear statement in a perfectly clear, limited and fully illuminated framework. It is an answer given with an eye on our immediate surroundings. But the question can also be meant differently and the questioner might not be satisfied with the answer given. "What is taking place here?"—One person is speaking, others are listening to the spoken word, and the hearers "understand" what is said; and among the hearers roughly the same thing happens; what is said is apprehended, weighed, considered, accepted or rejected, introduced into each individual's mind and way of thought. This question may aim at a scientific answer, it may be given such a meaning that physiology and psychology (awareness, understanding, learning, memorizing, forgetting, etc.) are called upon to answer and are sufficient for the task. And that answer would certainly be given in a world of wider and deeper dimensions than the former answer, that was purely technical. But the various scientific answers are not given with reference to the whole of reality; they could be given without bringing in "God and the world". Yet, if the question "what are we doing here and now?" is intended philosophically, it is impossible to answer without bringing in "God and the world". To ask the question philosophically is to ask about the essential nature of knowledge, of truth or perhaps only of teaching. What in fact do we really mean by teaching? One man will maintain that no one can really teach, just as in the case of good health it is not the doctor who performs the cure, but nature whose healing powers the doctor has simply liberated (perhaps). Another man will maintain that it is God and God only who teaches one inwardly—using the occasion of human teaching. And along comes Socrates and says that the teacher only induces the learner to remember "and to win knowledge from out of himself"; "there is no such thing as learning, one only remembers once again."[14] Yet another man comes along maintaining that we are all faced by or face the same reality: the teacher only points it out, the learner, the hearer, then sees it for himself.

"What are we doing here?" Something that takes place within the framework of a series of lectures, something organized; something moreover that can be grasped physiologically and psychologically and studied; something, too, between God and the world.

The distinctive mark of a philosophical question is, then, that it brings out what constitutes the essence of spirit: *convenire cum omni ente*, in harmony with everything that is. One cannot ask a philosophical question or think philosophically without bringing the whole of being into play, the totality of existing things, "God and the world".

[14] *Meno*, 85, 81.

III

It is appropriate to the human situation, as we have seen, not only for man to adapt himself to his environment, he must also address himself to the task of seeing the world as a whole. And the act of philosophizing means that he transcends his environment and steps forth into "the world".

That must not, of course, be understood to mean that there are, as it were, two distinct, separate spheres, and as though man could take leave of one and enter the other. Nor is it true that there are things which could be defined as belonging in his environment and others that do not occur in his environment, but occur in the other sphere, "the world". Obviously, our environment and the world (in the sense we have given these terms) are not distinct and separate spheres of reality—as though by asking a philosophical question one moved from the first to the second. A man philosophizing does not look away from his environment in the process of transcending it; he does not turn away from the ordinary things of the workaday world, from the concrete, useful, handy things of everyday life; he does not have to look in the opposite direction to perceive the universal world of essences. On the contrary, it is the same tangible, visible world that lies before him upon which a genuine philosophical reflection is trained. But this world of things in their interrelationships has to be questioned in a specific manner: things are questioned regarding their ultimate nature and their universal essence, and as a result the horizon of the question becomes the horizon of reality as a whole. A philosophical question is always about some quite definite thing, straight in front of us; it is not concerned with something beyond the world or beyond our experience of everyday life. Yet, it asks what "this" really *is*, ultimately. The philosopher, Plato says,[1] does not want to know whether I have been unjust to you in this particular matter, or you to me, but what justice really is, and injustice; not whether a king who owns great wealth is happy or not, but what authority is, and happiness and misery—in themselves and ultimately.

Philosophical questions, then, are certainly concerned with the everyday things that are before our very eyes. But to anyone raising such a question the things "before his eyes" become, all at once, transparent, they lose their density and solidity and their apparent finality—they can no longer be taken for granted. Things then assume a strange, new, and deeper aspect. Socrates, who questioned men in this way, so as to strip things of their everyday character, compared himself for that reason to an electric fish that gives a paralyzing shock to anyone who touches it. All day and every day we speak of "my" friend, of "my" wife, of "my" house, taking for granted that we "have" or "own" such things; then all of a sudden we are brought to a halt: do we really "have" or "own" all these things? Can anyone have such things? And anyway, what do we mean here by "having" and "owning" something?

To philosophize means to withdraw—not from the things of everyday life—but from the currently accepted meaning attached to them, or to question the value placed upon them. This does not, of course, take place by virtue of some decision to differentiate our attitude from that of others and to

---

[1] *Theaetetus*, 175.

see things "differently", but because, quite suddenly, things themselves assume a different aspect. Really the situation is this: the deeper aspects of reality are apprehended in the ordinary things of everyday life and not in a sphere cut off and segregated from it, the sphere of the "essential" or whatever it may be called; it is in the things we come across in the experience of everyday life that the unusual emerges, and we no longer take them for granted—and that situation corresponds with the inner experience which has always been regarded as the beginning of philosophy: the act of "marveling".

"By all the gods, Socrates, I really cannot stop marveling at the significance of these things, and at moments I grow positively giddy when I look at them", as the young mathematician *Theaetetus* impulsively declares, after Socrates has brought him to the point of admitting his ignorance, with his shrewd and kindly, but staggering and astonishing questions—questions that stagger and astonish one with wonder. And then follows Socrates' ironical answer: "Yes, that is the very frame of mind that constitutes the philosopher, that and nothing else is the beginning of philosophy."[2] There, for the first time, in the *Theaetetus*, without solemnity or ceremony, almost "by the way", though fresh as dawn, appears the thought that has become a commonplace in the history of philosophy: the beginning of philosophy is wonder.

It is at this point that the thoroughly "unbourgeois" character of philosophy emerges—if I may for a moment, and without an altogether good conscience, make use of a terminology that has become all too common. Yet wonder really is unbourgeois. For what do we mean by saying, in a spiritual sense, that something is bourgeois? Above all, in the first

[2] Ibid., 155.

place, that a man accepts his environment defined as it is by the immediate needs of life, so completely and finally, that things happening cannot any longer become transparent; the great, wide, not to say deep, world which is at first sight invisible, the world of essences and universals, is not even suspected; nothing wonderful ever happens in this world, and wonder itself is unknown or lost. The narrow insensitive mind, that has become narrow through being insensitive, takes everything for granted. And what, in truth, is to be taken for granted? Are we to take our very existence for granted? Is the existence of "sight" or "perception" to be taken for granted? No one imprisoned in everyday life *can* ask such questions because, in the first place, he is unable to forget his immediate needs (not at any rate while in full possession of his senses, at very most in some half-stupefied state); whereas that is precisely what characterizes the man capable of wonder. Those who are struck by the deeper aspect of things find the immediate aims of life vanishing before them—even though only for so long as their vision of the face of the world moves them to wonder.

The unique and original relation to being that Plato calls "theoria" can only be realized in its pure state through the sense of wonder, in that purely receptive attitude to reality, undisturbed and unsullied by the interjection of the will. "Theoria" is only possible in so far as man is not blind to the wonderful fact that things are. For our sense of wonder, in the philosophical meaning of the word, is not aroused by enormous, sensational things—though that is what a dulled sensibility requires to provoke it to a sort of *ersatz* experience of wonder. A man who needs the unusual to make him "wonder" shows that he has lost the capacity to find the true answer to the wonder of being. The itch for sensation, even though disguised in the mask of *Bohème*, is a

sure indication of a bourgeois mind and a deadened sense
of wonder.

To perceive all that is unusual and exceptional, all that is
wonderful, in the midst of the ordinary things of everyday
life, is the beginning of philosophy. And that, as both Aristotle and Aquinas observe, is how philosophy and poetry
are related. And Goethe, in his seventieth year, ended one
of his short poems, *Parabase*, with the words: *Zum Erstaunen
bin ich da*, which might be rendered by saying "marvel is my
raison d'être." Ten years later Eckermann[3] records him saying
that "the very summit of man's attainment is the capacity to
marvel."

The philosopher and the poet are "unbourgeois" in so
far as they preserve a deep and strong sense of wonder, and
this fact naturally exposes them to the danger of losing their
foothold in the everyday world. Indeed it might almost be
said that "to be a stranger in the world" is their occupa-
tional disease (though of course there could no more be a
professional philosopher than there could be a professional
poet—for as we said, man *cannot* live permanently at such
heights). Wonder, however, does not make a man "able"—
it means, after all, to be profoundly moved and "shaken".
And those who undertake to live under the sign and constel-
lation "wonder" (why *is* there such a thing as being?) must
certainly be prepared to find themselves lost, at times, in the
ordinary workaday world. The man to whom everything is
an occasion of wonder will sometimes simply forget to use
these things in a workaday way.

But however that may be, it remains true that the capacity
to wonder is among man's greatest gifts. To Aquinas it even
appeared to offer proof that man could only find peace and

---

[3] [Johann Peter] Eckermann, Feb. 18, 1829.

rest in the contemplation of God; and conversely, because man's mind is ordained to knowledge of the first cause of the world, he is capable of wonder. Furthermore, Aquinas held that man's first experience of wonder sets his feet on the ladder that leads up to the beatific vision. And the truth that human nature is intended for no less an end is revealed in the fact that we are capable of experiencing the wonder of the creation, or quite simply that we are capable of wonder.

Wonder acts upon a man like a shock, he is "moved" and "shaken", and in the dislocation that succeeds all that he had taken for granted as being natural or self-evident loses its compact solidity and obviousness; he is literally dislocated and no longer knows where he is. If this were only to involve the man of action in all of us, so that a man only lost his sense of the certainty of everyday life, it would be relatively harmless; but the ground quakes beneath his feet in a far more dangerous sense, and it is his whole spiritual nature, his capacity to know, that is threatened.

It is an extremely curious fact that this is the only aspect of wonder, or almost the only aspect, that comes to evidence in modern philosophy, and the old view that wonder was the beginning of philosophy takes on a new meaning: doubt is the beginning of philosophy.

In one of Hegel's lectures on the history of philosophy[4] he speaks of Socrates' method and of how, in the dialogues, he excites his opponent to wonder *vis-à-vis* all that he had hitherto taken for granted. But, says Hegel, the confusion Socrates introduces into his opponent's mind is the principal thing: "that purely negative thing is the main point", and further, "confusion is what Philosophy must begin with, and it produces that by itself; one must doubt everything,

[4] Lecture 2. 69.

give up all one's assumptions, in order to receive it all (one's previous knowledge, etc.) back again by means of the concept." And the line of descent from this position to Windelband's famous *Introduction to Philosophy* is unbroken. There, Windelband translates "θαυμάζειν" boldly as "Irrewerden des Denkens as sich selbst",[5] "Thought becoming confused at itself." Chesterton, be it said by the way, made a very pertinent comment on all such attempts to do without assumptions when he said that there was a particular form of madness which consisted in losing everything but one's reason.

But does the true sense of wonder really lie in uprooting the mind and plunging it in doubt? Doesn't it really lie in making it possible and indeed necessary to strike yet deeper roots? The sense of wonder certainly deprives the mind of those penultimate certainties that we had up till then taken for granted—and to that extent wonder is a form of disillusionment, though even that has its positive aspect, since it means being freed from an illusion; and it becomes clear that what we had taken for granted was not ultimately self-evident. But further than that, wonder signifies that the world is profounder, more all-embracing and mysterious than the logic of everyday reason had taught us to believe. The innermost meaning of wonder is fulfilled in a deepened sense of mystery. It does not end in doubt, but is the awakening of the knowledge that being, *qua* being, is mysterious and inconceivable, and that it is a mystery in the full sense of the word: neither a dead end, nor a contradiction, nor even something impenetrable and dark. Rather, mystery means that a reality cannot be comprehended *because* its light is ever-flowing, unfathomable, and inexhaustible. And that is what the wonderer really experiences.

[5] [Wilhelm] Windelband, *Einleitung in die Philosophie*, p. 6 (1923).

It will now be seen that wonder and philosophy are related in a far more essential way than might, at first sight, be
supposed from the saying that "wonder is the beginning of
philosophy." Wonder is not just the starting point of philosophy in the sense of *initium*, of a prelude or preface. Wonder is the *principium*, the lasting source, the *fons et origo*, the
immanent origin of philosophy. The philosopher does not
cease "wondering" at a certain point in his philosophizing
—he does not cease to wonder unless, of course he ceases
to philosophize in the true sense of the word.

The inner form of philosophizing is virtually identical
with the inner form of wonder. And since we have asked
"what we mean by philosophizing" we must now inquire
more closely into the nature of wonder.

There is something about wonder which is both positive
and negative. The negative aspect is this: to wonder is not
to know fully, not to conceive absolutely; it means not to
know what is behind it all; it means, as Aquinas says, "that
the cause of that at which we wonder is hidden from us."[6]
And so, to wonder is not to know, not to know fully, not to
be able to conceive. To conceive a thing, to possess comprehensive and exhaustive knowledge of a thing, is to cease to
wonder. It cannot therefore be said that God "wonders"—
because the knowledge of God is perfect. But, furthermore,
to wonder is not merely not to know; it means to be inwardly aware and sure that one does not know, and that one
understands oneself in not knowing. And yet it is not the
ignorance of resignation. On the contrary to wonder is to
be on the way, *in via*; it certainly means to be struck dumb,
momentarily, but equally it means that one is searching for
the truth. In the *Summa Theologica*[7] wonder is defined as

---

[6] *Quaest. disp. de potentia Dei*, 6, 2.
[7] *Summa Theologica*, I-II, 32, 8.

the *desiderium sciendi*, the longing for knowledge, an active desire for knowledge. Although to wonder means, as we have said, not to know, it does not mean that we are, in a kind of despair, resigned to ignorance. Out of wonder, says, Aristotle,[8] comes joy. In this he was followed by the Middle Ages: *omnia admirabilia sunt delectabilia*,[9] so that joy and wonder are produced by the same things. Perhaps one might risk the following proposition: Wherever there is spiritual joy, wonder will also be found; and wherever the capacity for joy exists the capacity for wonder will be found. The joy that accompanies wonder is the joy of the beginner, of the mind and spirit that is always open to what is fresh, new, and as yet unknown.

In its fusion of positive and negative, of ignorance on the way to further knowledge, wonder reveals itself as having the same structure as hope, the same architecture as hope —the structure that characterizes philosophy and, indeed, human existence itself. We are essentially *viatores*, on the way, beings who are "not yet". Who could claim to possess the being intended for him? "We are not", says Pascal, "we hope to be". And it is because the structure of wonder is that of hope that it is so essentially human and so essential to a human existence.

The philosophy of antiquity looked upon wonder as decisively and exclusively human. The absolute spirit does not wonder because untouched by the negative, for there is no ignorance in God. Only a being who does not know fully can wonder. But equally animals can have no sense of wonder because, as Aquinas says, "the sensual soul is not drawn to undertake the search for causes",[10] because the positive element in "the structure of wonder" (corresponding to

---

[8] *Rhetoric*, 1, 2.
[9] *Summa Theologica*, I-II, 32, 8.
[10] *Summa contra Gentes*, 4, 33.

hope) is absent: the desire for knowledge. It is only someone who *does not yet* know fully who "wonders". Wonder,
in fact, was accepted so instinctively as essential to a human life that in the quarrels and discussions that centered
on Christological doctrine there was an argument in favor
of the full humanity of Christ which might be called "an
argument from wonder". Arius had denied the divinity of
Christ; whereas Apollinaris put forward the thesis that the
eternal Logos had taken the place of the spiritual soul in
Christ and had immediately assumed a human body. We are
not concerned here with the theological side, though it is
in this kind of theological connection that one finds the traditional doctrine of being expressing itself "under oath",
as it were. In his argument against the teaching of Apollinaris that Christ did not possess the full humanity of body
and soul (but of body only) Thomas Aquinas argues, among
other things, from wonder: we are told in Holy Scripture,
in the story of the centurion (Luke 7:9), that "Christ won-
dered": "Lord I am not worthy, say but the word . . .", upon
which, the Gospel tells us, "Jesus heard and marveled"—
εθαύμασεν. But if Jesus could "marvel", Aquinas says,[11] we
must suppose the presence of that which is capable of marvel, of the *mens humana*, the human mind, of the spiritual
soul in addition to the presence of the Divine Word and the
sensual soul (both of which are, as we have seen, not capable
of "wonder"). Only a spiritual capacity for knowledge that
does not know everything it knows at once and perfectly
is capable of becoming gradually aware of the deeper and
more essential world behind the sensual, physical world—
only the human spirit is capable of wonder.

It is this distinctively human gift which is the mark of

[11] Ibid.

philosophy. The gods, we are told by Diotima in the *Symposium*,[12] do not philosophize; neither gods nor fools, for "the really damaging thing about stupidity is its self-satisfaction." "Who then, Diotima, I [Socrates] asked, who then philosophizes, if neither the wise nor the foolish philosophize? And to that she answered: It must surely be clear, even to a child, that it is those who are between the two, in the middle." The "middle" is the truly human sphere. The truly human thing is neither to conceive or comprehend (like God), nor to harden and dry up; neither to shut oneself up in the supposedly clear and enlightened everyday world, nor to resign oneself to remaining ignorant, not to lose the childlike suppleness of hope, the freedom of movement that belongs to those who hope.

And so the man who philosophizes and wonders is ultimately superior to one who submits to the despairing narrowness of indifference. For the former hopes! On the other hand, he is inferior to one who knows and comprehends, who finally possesses truth. Again, to wonder, to philosophize, means to hope!

It is, among other things, because it has the same structure as hope, that philosophy is radically different from the sciences. In philosophy and in science, the object is regarded in a radically different manner. The questions which science asks can all of them, in principle, be fully answered, or at any rate they are not unanswerable in principle. The cause of a specific infection will, or could, one day be given. In principle it will one day be possible to say: it has now been definitely, scientifically established that this and nothing else is the case. A philosophical question, on the other hand, can never be finally answered and disposed of—for instance

---

[12] *Symposium*, 204.

"what *is* this, ultimately?" or "what is illness?" or "what is knowledge?" or "what is man?" "No philosopher", we find Aquinas saying,[13] "has ever been able to grasp the being of a single fly", though, to be sure, it is counterbalanced by the other statement that in knowledge, the mind drives forward to the essence of things.[14] The object of philosophy is given to the philosopher "in hope". And here Dilthey's words might be recalled: The demands made upon anyone philosophizing, he wrote, are quite unrealizable. A physicist is a delightful reality, useful to himself and to others; the philosopher, like the saint, exists only in the ideal.[15]

The sciences, it could be said, cease of their nature to wonder—to the extent to which they attain results. The philosopher, however, never stops "wondering".

This gives us a clear picture of the greatness and the frontiers of science, and simultaneously the rank and questionableness of philosophy. True enough, in itself it is nobler to live under the open sky. But no man can stand it uninterruptedly. True enough, too, a question aimed at the universe as a whole and at the ultimate essence of things, is higher in rank than any scientific question. Only . . . the answer is quite simply not within our reach in the same way that the answers to a scientific question are.

Since the very beginning philosophy has always been characterized by hope. Philosophy never claimed to be a superior form of knowledge but, on the contrary, a form of humility, and restrained, and conscious of this restraint and humility in relation to knowledge. The words philosopher and philosophy were coined, according to legend—and the

[13] Commentary on the Apostles' Creed.

[14] *Summa Theologica*, I-II, 31, 5.

[15] [Wilhelm] Dilthey's letters to Count Paul Yorck von Wartenburg 1877–1897, p. 39 (Halle 1923).

legend is of great antiquity—by Pythagoras in explicit contrast to the words *sophia* and *sophos*: no man is wise, and no
man "knows"; God alone is wise and all-knowing. At the
very most a man might call himself a lover of wisdom and a
seeker after knowledge—a philosopher. Plato speaks in the
same tone in the *Phaedrus*[16] where he asks what we ought
to call Solon and Homer; and Socrates there decides that
"to call him wise seems to me, O Phaedrus, altogether too
much, for it is only applicable to a God; but a philosopher,
one who loves and seeks wisdom, or something of the kind,
seems to me suitable."

These stories are, of course, well known. But we are
prone to regard them as mere anecdotes, as no more than
rather special forms of expression. Yet it seems to me that
we ought to pay close heed to the statement being made in
this etymological aside on the meaning of the term "philosopher".

But just what is that statement?

There are two things to note. The first point is that we
do not possess knowledge or wisdom which is the end and
aim of philosophical inquiry; and moreover, that not only
do we not possess it at the moment, or by chance, but on
the contrary, that we *cannot* in fact have it, and that we are
dealing with a perpetual "not yet".

To inquire about the essence of a thing implies a claim to
comprehension of it. Now, to comprehend a thing means,
according to Aquinas, to know it as fully and as completely
as it can be known; it means to transform all that can be
known into knowledge, to know something through and
through, to the utmost limits of its knowability.[17] But there

---

[16] *Phaedrus*, 278.
[17] Commentary on St. John's Gospel.

is absolutely nothing that man can know in this way, in the strict sense of the word "comprehend". No question concerning the essence of things, and that means no philosophical question, can, therefore, be answered in the exact sense in which it is asked. Philosophy, in fact, aims at a type of wisdom which is unattainable, though not, of course, in such a way that it has no relation whatsoever to its aim. It is simply that wisdom is the object of philosophy, but as lovingly sought, and never fully possessed.

That is the first thing expressed by the word philosophy as it was used by Pythagoras, Socrates and Plato. This meaning was adopted by Aristotle and developed further in his *Metaphysics*. It subsequently passed from Aristotle, though with some variation, to the great medieval thinkers. Aquinas' commentary on the *Metaphysics* of Aristotle, for instance, contains some very surprising and penetrating remarks on this theme. Among other things, he says that because wisdom is sought for its own sake, it cannot be the absolute possession of man. The information brought to us by the sciences, on the other hand, is fully and completely possessed; though this information is (of its nature) only a means; it never can satisfy us so that we desire it for its own sake. That which can satisfy us fully, and which we consequently desire for its own sake, is precisely what is given us in hope: "the wisdom which is sought for its own sake", Aquinas says, "is something which cannot become man's possession"; that wisdom, he goes on to say, is really only given to man in the form of a loan—*sicut aliquid mutuatum.*[18]

Philosophy, then, can only be said to "possess" its object, to "have" its proper object in the act of searching lovingly for it. That is a very important point, and one that is by

---

[18] Commentary on the *Metaphysics*.

no means universally accepted. Hegel, for example, seems to take special pains to contradict this conception of philosophy in the preface to the *Phenomenology of Spirit* where he tells us that his aim is to do what he can to enable philosophy to cease being called love of wisdom, and become real knowledge. That would be to formulate a claim that, in principle, goes beyond anything possible to man—a claim that occasioned Goethe's ironic dismissal of Hegel and philosophers of his sort with the words: "these gentry think they lord it over God, Soul and World, though no one can comprehend what it all means."[19]

The original meaning of the word philosophy, and its original implications too, contain a second idea that is only rarely given explicit appreciation. The legendary words of Pythagoras, the *Phaedrus* of Plato, and Aristotle, all contrast the *human philosophos* and the *divine sophos*.

Philosophy, then, is not the loving search for any kind of wisdom; it is concerned with wisdom as it is possessed by God. Aristotle actually calls metaphysics, the most philosophical part of philosophy, "the divine science", because it deals with a wisdom that is only fully possessed by God.[20]

This second point, expressed in the original definition of philosophy, has more than one aspect. In the first place it emphasizes the notion that philosophy cannot fully comprehend its objects; the frontier that is here indicated is further defined as being the frontier between God and man: man can no more possess that particular wisdom than he can cease to be man. Furthermore, it means that philosophy implies a relation to theology; philosophy, if one may use the metaphor, is trained on theology, and this direction of

[19] In a letter to Zelter, Oct. 27, 1827.
[20] *Metaphysics*, 983a.

thought toward theology is part and parcel of philosophy. The original conception of philosophy has a window open on to theology. And that, as everyone knows, is clean contrary to the current notion of philosophy. The decisive mark of modern philosophy on its own showing is that it has cut itself off from theology and has become entirely independent of faith and tradition. And there is a third point expressed in the original conception of philosophy: the refusal to consider itself a theology, a doctrine of salvation.

Now what is meant by "wisdom as it is possessed by God"? The conception of wisdom underlying that phrase is the following: "Wisdom can only be attributed without qualification to him who knows the highest cause"[21] —where cause does not, of course, mean simply "efficient cause", but above all implies "final cause".

"To know the highest cause", then, does not mean to know the cause of some particular thing, but to know the cause of everything and of all things: it means to know the "whither" and the "whence", the origin and the end, the plan and the structure, the framework and the meaning of reality. It means to know "the world" and its highest cause. Knowledge of this kind, in the sense of comprehensive knowledge, can only be possessed by God, the absolute Spirit. Only God can conceive the world as from a single point: as from himself as its one first cause. If "wisdom can only be attributed without qualification to him who knows the highest cause", then in that sense, God alone is wise.

To be sure, the aim of philosophy is to understand reality as from a single principle. And essentially speaking, philosophy is "on the way", *in via*, to this aim, loving, seeking and hoping, as we said, but at the same time too, incapable

---

[21] *Summa Theologica*, II-II, 9, 2.

of definitely attaining its aim. If we are to retain the original meaning of the word philosophy we must never forget to hold firmly to both parts of the definition.

Among other things, it can now be seen how this conception of philosophy makes a rationalistic interpretation of the world, deduced from a single principle, and from the first cause, quite simply inconceivable. In other words a complete and closed "system" of philosophy is not possible. The claim to expound the world in a formula, or to have a formula with which to explain the world, is quite simply unphilosophic or pseudo-philosophy.

And yet Aristotle, in the *Metaphysics*, looks upon philosophy as the supreme science,[22] supreme because of its aim, because it aims at knowing the first cause of all things— even though its aim may only be attainable in the guise of hope or as a loan. In his commentary on this passage in the *Metaphysics*, Aquinas remarks that: "The little that is won here (in metaphysics) weighs more than all that is won in all the other sciences."[23]

It is because of the ambivalent structure of philosophy, because "marveling" sets one on a road that never ends, because the structure of philosophy is that of hope, that to philosophize is so essentially human—and in a sense to philosophize means living a truly human life.

---

[22] *Metaphysics*, 983a.
[23] Commentary on the *Metaphysics*, 1, 3.

IV

In the act of philosophizing, man's relationship to being as a whole is realized—he is face to face with the whole of reality; that was how we defined it. But long *before* the appearance of philosophy on the historical scene, from time immemorial, man has always had a given interpretation of the world and a meaning to attach to reality—"long before", "from time immemorial". This interpretation, this tradition, whether as teaching or as stories, was moreover concerned with the world as a *whole*.

"From time immemorial" man has been born into a doctrinal religious tradition offering an image of the world in its totality. An essential aspect of these traditions is that they existed and were valid "from time immemorial"—long before any philosophy or interpretation of reality had been built upon experience.

Some theologians have held that these primitive traditions can be traced back to a first, original revelation, traced back to a communication granted to mankind "in the beginning", to an unveiling of the meaning of the world as well as of the whole history of mankind, a revelation overgrown and encrusted with accretions but still surviving in the myths and traditions of all peoples. This is not the place to pursue this particular train of thought.

The important thing for our present purpose is to grasp that the great originators of Western philosophy, on whose thought it still largely lives, Plato and Aristotle, not only found and recognized a "traditional" interpretation of the

world alive and vigorous—they accepted it as their starting point when they began to philosophize. "The ancients
knew the truth, and if we were to discover it why should we
bother with the opinions of man?"[1] And how often, elsewhere, Plato speaks of this or that doctrine as having been
"handed down by the ancients", and therefore as not only
worthy of respect, but as unimpeachably and surpassingly
true: in a word, as sacred. "God, as the ancient doctrine
tells us, holds the beginning, the end and the middle of all
things in his hands, and leads them according to their nature and for the best", Plato writes in the *Laws*,[2] as an old
man. And similarly, Aristotle, in the *Metaphysics*,[3] says that
"to us, who come afterward, it has been handed down by
our forefathers and the ancients, that the whole of nature is
surrounded by the divine."

It is very important that it should be seen and understood
that the great paradigmatic figures of Western philosophy
are "believers" in relation to an existing interpretation of
the world, handed down by tradition. It is important because, under the impulse of a rationalistic and "progressive"
doctrine, the history of philosophy as it has been written in
modern times, does the exact reverse and sets the beginning
of philosophy at the moment when thought cut itself free
from tradition: philosophy, it is assumed, being the "coming
of age" of reason, of the *ratio*, and its emancipation from the
tutelage of tradition. Rebellion against *religious* tradition is
regarded as the very core of Western philosophy. And what
is more, this is supposed to be clearly apparent from the
history of Greek philosophy: the pre-Socratics, the philosophers of Asia Minor, are looked upon as almost Voltairian

[1] *Phaedrus*, 274.
[2] *Laws*, 7, 15.
[3] *Metaphysics*, 1074b.

figures fighting the battle of "enlightenment", when in fact recent research tends to show that Homeric mythology (so sharply criticized by the pre-Socratics from Thales to Empedocles) was itself a sort of "enlightened" theology, in opposition to which the pre-Socratics wished to return to a more primitive, "traditional" pre-Homeric theology.

The first spring of Western philosophy, never to be recaptured, appears to show, on the contrary, that philosophy has always been preceded by a traditional interpretation of the world—a tradition which supplied the spark that set philosophy on fire.

But Plato goes even further. Not only does he say that there is a tradition "handed down by the ancients", which ought to be honored by anyone who philosophizes. He is also convinced that the "wisdom of the ancients" is ultimately of divine origin: "Knowledge came down to us like a flame of light, as a gift from the gods, I am convinced, brought to us by the hand of some unknown Prometheus from a divine source—and the ancients, being better than we are, and nearer to the gods, handed this tradition down to us." That is what Plato says in the *Philebus*, in connection with the doctrine of ideas.[4]

According to Plato, "wisdom, as it is possessed by God", had become known and accessible to us in some way or other, *before* our search for wisdom began: before man began to philosophize. Deprived of this prior counterpoint, of this divine wisdom that in some way or other enlightens us like a gift, prior to all our own efforts at thought —deprived of this counterpoint, philosophy considered as the loving search for "wisdom as it is possessed by God" is utterly unthinkable—although, on the other hand, it is this

[4] *Philebus*, x, 16.

very fact which expresses the independence and self-reliance of philosophy. That is to say, the independence of philosophy *vis-à-vis* what has always been said and revealed "from time immemorial", that is, the tradition that comes down from divine revelation, lies in the fact that philosophy begins by considering visible, concrete things and the realities of experience; begins from the bottom, questioning things that are met with in everyday life, that always seem more wonderful to those who are searching for wisdom, and always reveal new depths of wonder—whereas, what has already been revealed is essentially prior to experience and to experience assimilated into thought: it is *not* a "result" wrung from experience, but a gift, something that has always been said.

This raises the question of the relation of philosophy to theology—theology in the large sense of the word, as the interpretation of that which is revealed. To simplify for a moment—though I do not think it is an oversimplification —the relation of theology and philosophy as it emerges in Plato and the whole of Greek philosophical thought comes more or less to this: Theology is always prior to philosophy, and not in a merely temporal sense, but with respect to inner origin and their relationship in that origin. Philosophical inquiry starts with a given interpretation of reality and of the world as a whole; and in that sense, philosophy is intimately connected, not to say bound, to theology. There is no such thing as a philosophy which does not receive its impulse and impetus from a prior and uncritically accepted interpretation of the world as a whole. It is in the field of theology, and quite independently of experience and previously to it, that the object of man's desire—"wisdom as possessed by God"—becomes visible, and it is this aim which supplies the impulse and guides the course of philosophical inquiry in its loving search as it moves through the world of experience.

That, however, does not mean to say that the theologian possesses what the philosopher is searching for. In his distinctive capacity as the guardian and interpreter of tradition, the theologian does not, as such, possess the knowledge of being charactcristic of thc gcnuine philosopher. The revelation which teaches us that the world is created by the Logos, is certainly a statement that also concerns the whole structure of reality; but the theologian whose business it is to preserve, defend and clarify the meaning of that statement in the context of tradition as a whole, does not, by that fact alone, acquire the worldly knowledge of the philosopher that derives from the concrete consideration of the things of this world. On the other hand, the philosopher who reflects upon the things of this world in the light of the revealed doctrine of the Logos, will attain to knowledge that would otherwise remain hidden from him, though the knowledge he gains will not be theological knowledge but demonstrable knowledge, philosophical knowledge of things in themselves.

The original concept of philosophy is characterized by its freedom from prejudice *vis-à-vis* theology, at least in so far as Plato is concerned. Plato would indeed have been astonished had anyone asserted that he had overstepped the limits of "pure" philosophy and trespassed into the field of theology—in the *Symposium*,[5] for instance, where Aristophanes is allowed to suggest a grotesque, almost farcical story of the first men. Originally, he says, men were round, with four arms and four legs, and double sexed; they were, he continues, subsequently cut in half (like pears ready for bottling) and now consequently they are all in search of their

---

[5] *Symposium*, 189f.

"other half", and this impulse is the essence of Eros, "the
desire and pursuit of the whole." But in spite of its farcical
details, the fundamental structure of this story is that in the
beginning our nature was healthy and unimpaired; but in
course of time man was driven by "hybris", by the consciousness of his great powers and still "greater thoughts",
to trespass upon the divine. As a punishment for this over-
weening pride, for wishing to be like gods, men lost their
original perfection, their completeness, though they were
left with hope: Eros is the desire of man to recapture his
original state of perfection, and perhaps the power which
really will fulfill this desire—"if we honor the gods".

That is undoubtedly not philosophy, nor is it a "result"
which could be reached by thought alone and the experience
of reality. But is it not, because Plato ponders the question
"what is Eros, ultimately?", at the same time allowing full
weight to the answer given by religious tradition—is it not,
perhaps, because of this conjunction of philosophy and theology (so characteristic of the Platonic dialogue), that to read
him is still to experience something intimately concerned
with man? Is that not really the source of the universal appeal of the dialogues, and the reason why they answer so
completely to the whole of man's nature?

And consequently, it is impossible to pursue a philosophy
that is consciously and radically divorced from theology—
and at the same time invoke the name of Plato. To philosophize in the manner of Plato, or with any claim to continue
the tradition of Plato, can only be done upon a theological
ground base and with a full consciousness of that counterpoint. No one can seriously inquire into the cause of all
things (and that is what happens in philosophy), and for
the sake of arbitrary methodical tidiness, simultaneously ex-

clude the existing religious tradition where it touches upon these basic themes—unless he no longer accepts the account given by tradition. What cannot seriously be done, is to accept tradition, we believe it, and then set it aside in order to philosophize.

The question then naturally arises, where nowadays the legitimate pre-philosophical tradition is to be found. What is the present-day form of what Plato[6] calls "the gift of the gods, brought down to us by some unknown Prometheus"? The answer to that question is that since the extinction of the classical world, there exists no pre-philosophical tradition relevant to the world as a whole, except the Christian tradition. There is no theology in the Western world of today, unless it be the Christian. Where, indeed, is there such a thing as a non-Christian theology, in the full sense of the word?

This means to say that if the claims and the requirements of Plato are to be honored, in the Christian aeon, philosophy can only be pursued as the counterpoint to Christian theology. "How is a Christian philosophy possible?" is a far less difficult question to answer than the question "How is a non-Christian philosophy possible?"—assuming, always, that we understand by philosophy all that Plato understood by it.

Obviously, this does not mean that a man has only to be a Christian, or to accept the Christian tradition, in order to become a philosopher without further ado—for that means, after all, to inquire deeply into the nature of things, and is linked to a man's vision of the world and dependent on his natural genius. Nor should this be understood to mean

[6] *Philebus*, 16.

that the only vital philosophy is a Christian philosophy. One can also philosophize vigorously in opposition to Christianity: but Christianity can only be replaced or supplanted, in this respect, by another belief, however carefully it may be decked out as purely "rational"—for rationalism has its own creed. And in that case, the structure of philosophy, as Plato understood it, as the counterpart to faith, is still retained. (If the religious tradition were to wither away altogether, so that words like God, Logos, and Revelation no longer conveyed any meaning, philosophy, too, would cease to grow.)

The life and soul of philosophy, and the tension that goes with it, depend upon its retaining what I have called its contrapuntal relation to theology. That is where it strikes root and where it draws the salt of the existential. If Heidegger's philosophical work has had such a stimulating effect, it is because philosophy had become a shriveled-up, intellectual discipline, the preserve of specialists in the worst sense of the word, and had lost all touch with theological themes (this was partially true even of so-called Christian philosophers). The explosive character of Heidegger's philosophy on the other hand is simply due to the fact that it asks challenging questions, and his questions are challenging because their source and impetus is theological, and so too should their answers be—though it is true that the theological answer is flatly rejected by Heidegger. But quite suddenly, once again, one could taste the salt of theology on one's tongue.

The same thing is happening nowadays in France to an extent and in a sense that is no mere fashion: "existentialist" atheism is by no means a "pure" philosophy, nor is it even "scientific": it is a theological position and brings to philosophy an essentially theological dimension—so that although it is not of course any more true, since it is concerned with a pseudo- or anti-theology, it is quite certainly more vital and deeply concerns the real man in us—because it is concerned with the whole, which is how we defined philosophy.

"Atheistical existentialism", writes Jean-Paul Sartre, "concludes from the non-existence of God that there is a being which exists and is not defined by any higher will than its own: that being is man"—and nobody, surely, will accept that as a philosophical thesis and not as a theological thesis, an article of faith even. But it does force thought and thinker on to the theological plane; and that is the type of counterpoint that makes for vital, vigorous philosophizing.

On the other hand, to be vital and true, philosophy must be the counterpoint to a true theology, and that, *post Christum natum*, means Christian theology. But to repeat, that does not mean to say that philosophizing allegedly referring to Christian theology is automatically vital and true. What it does mean is this: a philosophy at once vital and true either does not come into existence at all—and it is perfectly possible that we shall have to wait in vain—or if it does arise then it can only be a Christian philosophy—in the above sense.

That is not—need I say—a "purely" philosophical statement. But it is part and parcel of the philosophy that considers itself in terms of its origins, and sees itself as a loving search for "wisdom as God possesses it". Theoretically and methodologically, we can set aside a separate confine for "pure" philosophy and its ideas. But practically, in real life, it cannot be done. By the nature of the philosophical act, the person engaged in philosophizing cannot help overstepping the boundaries of "pure" philosophy and taking a theological position. He cannot help it because philosophizing is a fundamentally human relationship to reality and is only possible if our whole human nature is involved—and that necessarily involves the adoption of a definite position with respect to ultimate things.

This attempt to answer the question "what do we mean by philosophizing?" would not be complete without a brief reference to the notion of a Christian philosophy, though of course with no sort of claim to exhaust that many-sided problem or even to throw light on its main outlines.

To begin with, it is very necessary to contradict the widely held opinion that Christian philosophy, (or "a" Christian philosophy) can be distinguished from a non-Christian philosophy by the fact (among other things) that a Christian philosophy is ready with all the answers. That is not so. Although Christian philosophy takes shape as the counterpoint to unquestioned certainties, it is Christian philosophy which most fully grasps and expresses a truly philosophical sense of "wonder", with its source in ignorance. One of the great thinkers of our time, whose thought is inspired by Aquinas, has written that the characteristic of Christian philosophy, its distinguishing mark if you like, is not that it has all the answers up its sleeve, but that more than any other philosophy, it is inspired by the sense of mystery.[7] Even in the sphere of theology and of faith it is not after all true—in spite of the *certainty* of faith—that everything is clear to the believer and every problem already solved; on the contrary, as Mathias Joseph Scheeben said, the truths of Christianity are in a very special way inconceivable; the truths of reason are generally inconceivable; but the distinguishing mark of the truths of Christianity is that "in spite of being revealed, they still remain hidden."[8]

Someone might well ask, at this point, where the advan-

[7] Reginald Garrigou-Lagrange, O.P. *The sense of Mystery and the clair-obscur of the Spirit.*

[8] M. J. Scheeben, *Die Mysterien des Christentums*, p. 8 (1941).

tage of Christian philosophy lay, by comparison with a non-Christian philosophy, if it does not succeed in providing a full and adequate solution, if it does not hand one out the answer, and if the problem and question still remain. Perhaps, after all, the greater *truth* lies in seeing the world in its real character as a mystery, and as unfathomable. Perhaps reality is more truly and more profoundly apprehended when we experience being as a mystery, and as something which cannot be grasped in the hand in an all-embracing answer, or by means of some transparent and marvelously clear system. And that is the claim of Christian philosophy: to be truer —in its very recognition of the mysterious character of the world.

The consequence of this is not, indeed, to make philosophizing simpler. It appears, moreover, that Plato must have known and experienced that fact—if it is true to maintain[9] that he called philosophizing tragic *because* whoever philosophizes is always forced back upon myths, *because* no "purely" philosophical interpretation of the world could ever be complete and pursued to the point at which it formed a perfectly closed circle.

Christian philosophy is not, in fact, less intellectually arduous because, as one might be tempted to think, faith "illumines" reason. If it reaches back to theological arguments (as it does in the philosophy of Aquinas for example), that is not a way of making ready answers possible but a way of breaking down methodological barriers in order to give the most genuine philosophical impulse, the loving search for wisdom, a wider field—a way of introducing it into the realm of mystery, a realm which is by definition boundless, and to enter into that infinite realm is to enter on a path

[9] Gerhard Krüger, *Einsicht und Leidenschaft*, p. 301 (1939).

along which one can continue for ever without coming to an end.

On the other hand, the point of these theological truths about the world as a whole, and the meaning of human existence—one aspect of the function of theology in our salvation—is that it should hinder and resist the natural craving of the human spirit for a clear, transparent and definite system. That is what is meant by the old phrase that the truth of faith is the "negative norm" of philosophical thought.

This is not the way, in fact, to make philosophizing "simpler". Quite the contrary; no one could really suppose that it could be otherwise, and the Christian philosopher's task is more difficult than that of a thinker who does not feel himself bound by the truths of faith handed down by tradition. Something of this problem is felt in Hölderlin's *Hyperion* where he says: "Heart's wave could not curl and break beautifully into the foam of spirit, unless the ageless silent rock of destiny stood in its path."

It is the ageless, silent, immovable rock of revealed truth that hinders and prevents philosophical thought from flowing on uninterruptedly in the lifeless calm of a well-constructed channel. The complexity necessitated by this impediment is one of the distinguishing marks of Christian philosophy. For instance, a philosophy of history that reckons with the dominion of Antichrist at the end of time, with the fact that, humanly speaking, the history of mankind ends with a catastrophe, and in spite of this is not a philosophy of despair—a Christian philosophy of history in fact, cannot possibly arrive at an intellectually simple view of history; whereas the philosophy of "progress" becomes so simple (though one can no longer say that it is obvious!)—precisely because it omits the Apocalypse.

No, philosophical thought does not become simpler

merely because one can cling to the norm of Christian revelation. But—and this claim is self-evident to the Christian—a Christian philosophy is truer and does fuller justice
to reality. The opposition which revealed truth provides,
the impediment it puts in the way of philosophical thought,
is a fruitful opposition. The claim to which the Christian
philosopher submits is a severe one. One of the distinguishing marks of Christian philosophy is that it places itself under compulsion to endure that stress and strain, and is thus
carried beyond the sphere of purely intellectual difficulties.
It is a more complex task because it rejects formulae that
are clear and plausible *at the cost* of leaving things out, or of
ignoring or selecting from reality. The contemplation of revealed truth is a disturbing element in Christian philosophy
though a very fruitful one, for it means that the framework
of philosophy is widened, and, above all, it can never rest
satisfied with the flat, one-dimensional "harmonies" of rationalism. That is the moment when a Christian philosophy,
striking upon the rock of divine truth, foams and boils; and
that is its unique privilege.

Christian philosophy, then, is enriched by its contrapuntal relation to the truth of revelation. In this, we are assuming two things (as a *condicio sine qua non*); first of all that the
Christian character of the philosophy in question is genuine
and powerful, and secondly (this is so often overlooked by
Christians) that its *philosophical* character is genuine and powerful. (Maurice de Wulff's well-known history of medieval
philosophy ends with the words that Scholasticism did not
die from lack of ideas, but from lack of men!)

And so in this sense the "No" that theology opposes to
philosophical thought, the effect of theology as *norma nega-
tiva* is anything but "negative". For surely no one could describe as purely negative the fact that thought, from the very

outset, is prevented from falling into certain errors. The positive aspect only fully emerges in the fact that through the recognition of revealed truth, the human mind grasps certain philosophical truths though "in themselves" they could be attained and established by natural means. The statement that "states without justice are simply robber-bands" is certainly intelligible to natural reason, and yet is it no mere chance that it should not occur in a work on the philosophy of law but in a theological work, St. Augustine's *The City of God*.

The question may now perhaps be asked, whether after all we have said, philosophy is not really entirely superfluous for the Christian. Is not theology enough, or just simply faith? "Those who have a *Weltanschauung* and who are determined in no circumstances to relinquish it", Windelband says in his *Introduction to Philosophy*[10] (and what he says certainly applies to the Christian), "have no need whatsoever of philosophy". Now of course it is quite true that our salvation does not require us to philosophize; only one thing is necessary, and it is certainly not philosophy. The Christian does not and cannot await an answer from philosophy on the subject of his salvation, nor, of course, salvation itself. And so he cannot philosophize as though his salvation depended upon his understanding of the world. To lose oneself in philosophical problems, to identify oneself existentially, as it were, with them, though characteristic of all philosophizing that does not look beyond itself—and the more earnest and genuine the inquiry, the more characteristic it will be—is really foreign to the believer. It sometimes seems as though Aquinas' conviction that such a thing as "a comprehensive

---

[10] *Einleitung in die Philosophie*, p. 5.

understanding" of *anything* in the world is impossible, were tinged with delight and almost with humor.

Philosophy is as necessary and as superfluous as the natural perfection of the human being. As we saw, to philosophize is to realize the natural bent of the human mind and spirit toward the whole. But who could possibly calculate the precise degree of that necessity in individual cases?

And now one final thing: up till now we have spoken as though "Christianity" meant doctrine, statement, truth exclusively. We have spoken of the Christian philosopher in much the same way as one might speak of a Kantian philosopher—by which is meant someone whose philosophy is in agreement with that of Kant. But to say that a man is Christian in the act of philosophizing does not mean only that his point of view is that of Christianity considered as doctrine. For Christianity is essentially reality and not merely doctrine. The problem before a Christian philosophy does not therefore lie in harmonizing natural and supernatural knowledge theoretically; nor does it consist in the choice of the method to be adopted to that end. The point is that a man's existence should be so deeply rooted in the Christian reality, that his philosophy, too, should become, as a result, Christian. "The philosophy a man chooses", Fichte said, "depends upon the sort of man he is"—not an altogether happy way of expressing the thought, since that is not how things happen (one does not after all choose a philosophy as one would choose assorted chocolates). Still, what Fichte meant is clear enough, and very much to the point. Even where natural knowledge is concerned, the discovery of the truth is not merely a matter of hard thinking, and when the truth concerns the meaning of the world, a good brain is not enough: the whole human personality is involved.

Now, to be a Christian *is* a qualification of being, of the whole of a man's being, and the more he opens himself to it, the more completely will it inform and transform all his faculties, including his intelligence. This is not the place, nor is it my business, to speak in detail of these things. What has been said should be enough to show everyone something of the existential structure of a Christian philosophy. In Thomas Aquinas[11] we find a distinction, which sounds altogether modern, between two ways of knowing: between properly theoretical, conceptual knowledge, knowledge *per cognitionem* on the one hand, and knowledge *per connaturalitatem* on the other, knowledge based upon existential affinity. The first form gives one knowledge of something foreign, in the second form one knows what belongs to one. A moralist for instance, who is not necessarily a morally good man, judges the good in the first manner; a good man knows what goodness is in the second, *per connaturalitatem*— on the basis of a direct participation, of an inner sympathy, and the unerring scent of love, for it is love, as, likewise, Aquinas[12] goes on to say, which brings about *connaturalitas*, which makes something foreign into one's own.

Now, to speak with judgment about divine things in this manner, as of one's own, is only possible to him who, in the words of Denys the Areopagite, "is not only learned in the divine, but who has suffered it."[13]

The undiminished form of Christian philosophy will therefore only be realized by one who has not just "learnt" his Christianity, to whom it is not just "doctrine", with

[11] *Summa Theologica*, I, 1, 6; II-II, 45, 2.

[12] *Summa Theologica*, II-II, 45, 2.

[13] Dionysus Areopagitica, *De divinis nominibus*, 2, 4, quoted by Aquinas, *Summa Theologica*, II-II, 45, 2.

which his conclusions are brought into theoretical and conceptual agreement—but by one who lets Christianity become real in him, and thus makes these truths his own, not by knowledge alone, but through "suffering" and experiencing reality, the Christian reality—and then philosophizes on the meaning of life and the natural reasons and causes of the world.